Praise for *we the same*

"So visceral and vital that it takes one's breath away ... Reading this play gives me such quiet joy and, more importantly, hope for a better tomorrow."
—DEEPA MEHTA
Internationally acclaimed director of *Fire*, *Earth*, and *Water*

"Tôi muốn bày tỏ lòng biết ơn sâu sắc tới vở kịch we the same của Sangeeta Wylie, một tác phẩm đáng trân trọng và chân thật. Nhờ đó, nhiều thế hệ người Việt hiện giờ có thể nắm bắt được một mảnh ghép cần thiết về một thời kỳ đen tối, khi đồng bào của chúng tôi đã phải chọn lựa giữa nhân phẩm và sự sống còn. | I'd like to express my gratitude for Sangeeta Wylie's *we the same*, a significant and authentic piece. Many Vietnamese generations now hold a necessary piece of the puzzle about a grim period when our people had to choose between survival and dignity."
—NGUYEN MINH NGOC
Director, actor, and author of *Pearls of the Far East*

"In a world constantly transitioning from chaos, Wylie underscores that while some humans inflict harm, others embody healing. *we the same* illustrates this diverse human capacity amid adversity."
—CHARLIE WU
author of *Taiwan, The World's Answer*

"Inspired by a stirring true story, simultaneously epic and intimate. Sangeeta Wylie delivers a very impressive debut."
—ROBERT CHAFE
Governor General's Award–winning playwright and actor

"*we the same* never sensationalizes the refugee experience but rather humanizes it ... The play is awe-inspiring and will be eye-opening to many, most certainly anyone who is unfamiliar with the kind of astonishingly difficult journey the Truongs endured."
—GAIL JOHNSON
Stir Vancouver

"For those old enough to remember news stories of 'boat people' arriving, *we the same* helps to personalize and connect the dots between what happened 'over there' and their arrival here."
—JAY MINTER
On the List

T0203508

we the same

we the same

a play inspired by true events

by Sangeeta Wylie

Foreword by Deepa Mehta

Talonbooks

Talonbooks
9259 Shaughnessy Street, Vancouver, British Columbia, Canada v6p 6r4
talonbooks.com

Talonbooks is located on xʷməθkʷəy̓əm, Sḵwx̱wú7mesh, and səlilwətaɬ Lands.

First printing: 2024
Typeset in Minion
Printed and bound in Canada on 100% post-consumer recycled paper

Talonbooks acknowledges the financial support of the Canada Council for the Arts, the Government of Canada through the Canada Book Fund, and the Province of British Columbia through the British Columbia Arts Council and the Book Publishing Tax Credit.

LIBRARY AND ARCHIVES CANADA CATALOGUING IN PUBLICATION

Title: We the same / by Sangeeta Wylie ; preface by the author ; foreword by Deepa Mehta.
Names: Wylie, Sangeeta, author, writer of preface. |
Mehta, Deepa, 1949– writer of foreword.
Description: A play. | Includes bibliographical references. |
Includes some text in Vietnamese.
Identifiers: Canadiana 20230581218 | ISBN 9781772016161 (softcover)
Subjects: LCGFT: Drama.
Classification: LCC PS8645.Y42 W42 2024 | DDC C812/.6—dc23

*For Jean and May, and the millions of refugees
from the past, present, and future*

Dedicated to all those who have ever been othered ...

We are the foam,
floating on the vast ocean.
We are the dust,
wandering in endless space.
Our cries are lost
in the howling wind.

—THÍCH NHẤT HẠNH
"A Prayer for Land" (1977)
Call Me By My True Names:
The Collected Poems of Thich Nhat Hanh (2022)

Trigger Warning

This play makes reference to sexualized violence.

FOREWORD

"Art is not what mirrors reality, but a hammer that shapes it." My favourite quote about Art is this one by Bertolt Brecht. And never has it been more applicable than for Sangeeta Wylie's superb play *we the same*. Sangeeta takes a true and often-read, seen, and heard story and wields Brecht's hammer on it, changing it into something so visceral and vital that it takes one's breath away. The characterization of Hà, the lead, is a woman Wylie gives breadth to without once reducing her to a cliché. As a mother of six fleeing from Saigon after the civil war, Hà has innate wisdom. This with a combo of shoulder-shrugging matter-of-factness giving impact to her lines like "A mother knows herself by her children" or "Power not come from being smart. It come from gun. Smart people not want use the gun." This play, as the title suggests, is very particular to the female perspective of survival amidst horrendous conditions, but at the same time it's this particular quality that makes *we the same* universal. I read in its essence not only a mother-daughter story but also a political one. The havoc that decolonization has caused in the world has resonance not only in Wylie's totally authentic Vietnamese characters but also ones from my own history of the division of India into Pakistan and India, from Rwanda, Russia and Ukraine, Yemen, and now Palestine and Israel. Ultimately *we the same* reinforces not only the heart-rending echo of division but also the will of women like Hà, Kim, and Biên to survive. Reading this play gives me such quiet joy and, more importantly, hope for a better tomorrow.

—DEEPA MEHTA

Deepa Mehta's fee for this foreword has been donated to a charity of the playwright's choosing, the Dalhousie University Elizabeth F. Precious Endowment, which funds surgical care for children with cleft lip and palate in Việt Nam.

Top: Real-life inspirations Jean and her children at a refugee camp known as Camp Canada, a temporary holding centre for refugees awaiting transport to Canada. Kuala Lumpur, Malaysia, 1980. Photo credit: unknown

Bottom: Real-life inspirations Jean and Tom, Sài Gòn, Việt Nam, circa 1967–1968, prior to their marriage. Photo credit: unknown

THE MAKING OF SALAD ROLLS AND A PLAY

BY SANGEETA WYLIE

This is not my story. Yet it is, and must be all of our story.

The genesis of this play came over a dinner conversation with friends, in the spring of 2017. My friend May had made homemade peanut sauce to accompany her salad rolls, a Vietnamese dish I immediately recognized. While we had been friends for two years, somehow, we never had the "Where are you from?" conversation. Maybe this was due to a wave of new understanding that this question was hastily equating one's birthplace with their physical appearance. I've answered this question most of my life with "From here," only to be further asked, "Where are your parents from?"

In the most organic of ways and out of a desire to know more about May, I did ask her if she was from Việt Nam. This led to a conversation about her family, who had left Việt Nam in 1979 by boat. As May recounted the story, using only the scant details she was told rather than remembered herself, I learned about her mother and father's separation on the boats, about a woman with six children surviving a journey marked by pirate attacks, typhoons, a shipwreck onto a deserted island, and a year spent in refugee camps. I thought that if even one of these events had occurred in my lifetime, it would certainly have been traumatic. May's family had endured more than their share of adversity, and I felt an intense admiration for their strength to survive, somehow without too many scars.

Months prior to this conversation, I was approached by the artistic director of a local theatre to submit a proposal for their playwrights' lab. I thought of writing my own story of adversity, one that might create a role for me as an actor. However, the timing wasn't right and May's story tugged on my sleeve like a persistent child wanting to be heard. I listened to that little voice inside me and, rather haphazardly, put together a proposal that included two scenes and a working title: "The Boat People." I envisioned a framework of blurred reality and memory – that of a child contrasted with her mother's. The theatre accepted the proposal, and from there the play took on a momentum of its own.

After five months of research, interviews, and workshops, my first draft of "The Boat People" was completed. The play's first reading was held at Vancouver's Playwrights Theatre Centre on February 22, 2018, to a full house. I selected Asian Canadian actors from a list of headshots and short bios.

We had long discussions about what this history meant to the younger generations of Asian Canadians; the actors weren't all from Việt Nam but they felt a connection to the play's themes. "The Boat People" was selected for a second reading at the Roundhouse Community Arts and Recreation Centre, Vancouver, on May 15, 2018. There was a palpable feeling that this story was touching our audiences and cast alike. Actor Elizabeth Thai, who played Hà in every development phase straight through to the premiere production on November 3, 2021, at The Cultch in Vancouver, spoke of how much the play meant to her personally as a "boat person" herself. She wrote a letter of support for a grant application, that explained the reasons why the experience of the play was special and cited feedback from a diverse audience, including many Vietnamese Canadian people who didn't normally attend theatre. They were overflowing with praise about how accurate the story was and "how almost relieved they were that someone was finally telling their story with such honesty and integrity."[1] Many had remarked, Elizabeth wrote, that "this was not a story about the Vietnamese people told from the Western, outsider perspective that they so often experienced." She assessed that, "through tireless research, Sangeeta [had] made sure that 'The Boat People' [was] told from the perspective of the survivors, and the children of the survivors, and [rang] with an authenticity as if my own mother, father, or grandparent were recounting their own journey from Việt Nam." Another passage from Elizabeth's letter was particularly poignant:

I was so deeply moved by the reaction of the audience and the comments from them. I would like to share one particular exchange I had, with a Vietnamese woman who approached me after the show. At first, she was very shy, and just congratulated me on my performance and how much she enjoyed the show. As she talked, it was as though a flood gate opened up. She began to tell me her personal story of coming to Canada, how she had attempted to flee Việt Nam three times as a child, been caught and sent back, seen family members put in jail for attempting to leave, and finally coming over as a young adult. In her life here in Canada, she said she always felt like she didn't belong. Her Vietnamese friends told her she was not "Vietnamese enough," and her Canadian friends told her she was "not Canadian like them." In seeing the play, she gained insights into her past, her life, and how all of it had contributed to her sense

1   Elizabeth Thai, letter to the author, July 6, 2018. Quoted with permission.

of disconnection. She said she also saw how she was perpetuating that disconnectedness in her life now, with her husband, and sadly with her children ... [As a result of] viewing the play, she told me, she vowed to go home and share with her children her past experiences and build a closer relationship with them. It was one of the most moving conversations I've ever had with someone, and the fact that it came about out of our show made the whole experience even more memorable.[2]

Actress Elizabeth Thai beside the outfit she wore when she left Việt Nam at age two with her family in 1981. Photo credit: Keith Halak

---

2   Elizabeth Thai letter.

It took about two years, during a trip to Asia in April of 2019, to recognize my personal connection to the piece, which, in the meantime, found its title: *we the same*. ("The Boat People" being a holding title, *we the same* was birthed from a line within the play: "We the same now. Refugee." [act 2, scene 1]). At last the underlying story of a family being torn apart by unjust persecution hit home. If I had any thoughts of "Why me?," they were erased as I began to understand the parallels in my own life. Art chooses us. Buried deep inside, this was my own story and familial reconciliation, which would not have happened without this play. And Art creates connection: I fell in love with Việt Nam, her culture and people.

The first trip to Việt Nam changed me. Despite the overwhelming hardship this beautiful country has experienced at the hands of colonization, wars, sanctions, political unrest, and the lasting effects of Agent Orange, I was struck by how kind and generous the people were. I experienced a bare authenticity unlike anything I had seen in other places I'd visited. A simplicity in living that lacked pretension. It made me feel humble at once and taught me a very important lesson: to allow myself to surrender. Surrender my Western misconceptions and expectations, surrender my very self, in order to fully experience other people. I traced the journey of May's family, who inspired the play, travelling for five days to the Mekong with a translator, and an educator/historian originally from North Việt Nam, who had moved to the South after the war to teach modified social sciences courses. Visiting areas I had incorporated into the play, some factual and some enhanced by the work of literary license or research (such as the floating markets of Cái Răng, Cần Thơ, and Bạc Liêu), provided me with a greater sense of setting, which I had only imagined thus far. In Sóc Trăng, southern Việt Nam, we called without notice on one of the family's relatives: an eighty-year-old bamboo farmer who lived in a two-room thatched hut. I was struck by his elderly wife's reception of us. The mud floor was littered with cigarette butts; the room, crowded with all the furniture one might expect and then some, included a motorbike. And this beautiful woman, a grandmother, reached for her comb first, prior to uttering a greeting. Looking back at a photo, she didn't even have a mirror.

Although it's not portrayed in the play, we also went further south to the city of Cà Mau, which I was told is the mythological nose of Việt Nam, and a place where every Vietnamese is expected to make a pilgrimage at least once in their lifetime. A full day of driving on what felt like the ocean culminated with a boat ride in the black of night, along narrow waterways, to the country's southernmost tip, or what felt like the ends (or beginnings) of the earth. It was reminiscent of a scene from *Apocalypse Now*. There, at Homestay Đất Mũi Nguyễn Hùng, I encountered a woman who would transform the backstory of the character Biên. Dressed in loungewear I now recognize to be typical of what many Vietnamese women wear, she seemed intently focused on me, sharing stories, including her past attempts to become a mail-order bride. When I heard that she had asked if I "liked her", my writer curiosity was piqued: why was she so interested in me? Eventually, she asked if I'd be willing to "invest" in some land. Humouring her, I asked how much it would be. When she responded with something like twelve billion Vietnamese dongs (around seven hundred thousand Canadian dollars), I had to respectfully decline. I then realized her husband, a musician sitting opposite us, had been closely watching us the whole time. I imagine I was not the first tourist to be approached in this manner.

Cà Mau was also where I shook bamboo sticks, or "kau chim," referred to in act 1, scene 1, and act 2, scene 10. We matched the fallen numbered stick to the correlated written oracle in a fortune telling book and had great fun reading. I later visited a Buddhist temple in which the actual fortune-telling scrolls were kept instead of their book equivalents. Traversing along those watery pathways in Cà Mau, we found a whale shrine housed in a small hut. The Vietnamese practice of whale worship, known as Cá Ông, is intriguing; its origins are still mostly unknown. My historian companion mentioned a Cham fishermen dance related to whales. Researching this, I found that the Chams, these pre-Vietnamese people of Hindu, Buddhist, and Islamic faiths, performed a ritual dance during ocean storms to invoke the protection of Lord Shiva, God of whales. This had some resonance with a whales scene (act 1, scene 10) I had written in 2017, as well as with my Hindu faith. Through one of many coincidences that seemed to be leading me in the right direction, I later reached out to an old acquaintance who had taught me Bharatanatyam, a South Indian classical dance form. I hadn't spoken to her in over thirty years, and she was now in her eighties. I discovered that a dance I performed as a child had a similar spiritual mythology to the Cham ritual dance.

Back in Sài Gòn (now known as Hồ Chí Minh City), I attended a British Council panel led by interdisciplinary artist Nguyễn Thị Minh Ngọc on cải lương, a Vietnamese opera form, which, having languished in the 1980s, was now experiencing an intentional resurrection effort. Cải lương had been synonymous with southern culture, which the Vietnamese Communist Party aimed to reform in a bid to purify extravagances as well as remove non-socialist, Chinese-origin, themes from. This government control over thinking and belief extended to media, education, and religion, making it difficult to discover the South Vietnam I was searching for – not everything is available on Google. A female panelist who played the đàn tranh, a plucked zither, told me about how she had participated, extolling the instrument's use, in an international environmental forum in Delhi, India. The entrancing, nearly lost art form, cải lương, had been placed on my path, along with advocate Minh Ngoc, who became a cultural consultant on the play. While I considered for a time incorporating Vietnamese water puppetry that I'd observed in Hà Nội into the "Pirate Games" scene (act 1, scene 5), it was Minh Ngoc who later informed me that the art's North Vietnamese origin made it inappropriate for this South Vietnamese story. Minh Ngoc introduced me to the Broadway dancer turned film director Leon Le, her co-writer of *Song Lang*, a beautiful, award-winning film depicting a relationship between a cải lương performer and a hardened loan shark, that opened the 2019 Vancouver Queer Film Festival. Our shared personal stories and the film's depiction of cải lương during 1990's Sài Gòn continued to broaden my understanding of Vietnamese culture as it adjusted to political shifts. I knew that I wanted to incorporate both the đàn tranh and the đàn ghi ta (the Vietnamese guitar) into my play through Kim and Danh's characters, and once back in Vancouver, made inquiries of my then-consultant to source musicians to play one or both of these instruments.

Resuming my journey of remarkable meetings, I chanced upon a woman at an open-air market, who, hesitatingly, spoke of her relatives leaving by boat. Her fear of speaking openly about "the boat people" was palpable in her request to delete photographs of her. These kinds of experiences are not uncommon within a Communist country; indeed, my time in Việt Nam was purposefully relegated to experience rather than overt planning, to avoid any trouble. Memorably, I ate lunch with an ex-Việt Cộng female soldier, who regaled me with interesting war stories. There wasn't enough room to add such a fascinating character to the play. Following the cải lương panel I met a woman, a television host and actor, who was finishing her book on the 1975 fall of Sài Gòn. She was born that same year and had never experienced Sài Gòn before it was lost; yet, how she expressed her sadness was captivating. The daughter of a high-ranking communist, as a child she had, alongside her father, enjoyed the postwar privileges of attending the exclusive "foreigners' clubs", where a part of Sài Gòn continued to exist. She was a beautiful, enigmatic woman, and I was drawn to her like a sister. Figuring there must be a good live-jazz club in Sài Gòn, I had just asked my translator about finding one, when I received an email from this woman, inviting me to a club where a famous jazz saxophonist was to play. We watched this extraordinary musician at one point playing two saxophones at the same time, while talking about the Sài Gòn that once was. I affectionately dubbed her Miss Sài Gòn, since it seemed like she embodied the city, and that era. We have remained dear friends: on a recent visit to Việt Nam, her book had finally been published, and she gifted me a copy. (Now I just need to learn how to read Vietnamese fluently!) This woman introduced me to a young musician who contributed two musical recordings to the production, though I had dreams of him playing his đàn ghi ta live, on opening night.

If I learned how to surrender in Việt Nam, Malaysia taught me how to listen. It was there that I felt more at ease in conducting open interviews. I arranged to meet with several people: a veteran playwright, a dancer, a female actor, a journalist, nuns who ran the transit refugee camp nicknamed Canada Camp (see act 2, scene 8), workers at the Malaysian Red Crescent Society (a chapter of the Red Cross), Canadian embassy workers, and a United Nations High Commissioner for Refugees worker. At the Red Crescent's offices, I dug through the refugee registration cards, those "blue index cards" (act 2, scene 8), which were in massive disarray, eventually locating the card of a dear friend's deceased father. I was told that many Vietnamese experience intense reactions when they reunite with these "living documents." I sent a photo to my friend in Vancouver, who gratefully returned my text right away, feeling as though her father had reached her beyond the grave. I spent time at the National Archives of Malaysia, researching news articles, and found there were large gaps in the collection. A meeting with Eddin Khoo, a journalist, cultural advocate, and founder of the performance-arts NGO Pusaka, led to a wonderful friendship and years of philosophical discussions related to the play's themes and beyond. I absorbed much from our conversations on several Asian art forms, such as shadow play, shadow puppetry (known as wayang kulit in Malaysia), and mak yong (a ritualistic folk theatre form in Malaysia). Shadow puppetry, which I knew and loved from my own Indian culture where it originates, has a long history in several Southeast Asian countries. Coincidentally, I had already envisioned the use of shadows in certain scenes of the play, just like I had envisioned a dance for the "Whales" scene (act 1, scene 10); now I was finding justification for these ideas. The last leg of my trip was to Kuala Terengganu, Malaysia, to explore the beach where characters Hà and Bảo are separated, and then to the island of Pulau Bidong, tagged as one of the most densely populated places on earth in the late 1970s, with, at its peak, about forty thousand refugees inhabiting the one-square-kilometre island.

These areas added invaluable visuals and a chance to interview local people who remembered the Vietnamese refugees.

The trip to Asia, an intentional foray into cultures and art forms, was the first of two in 2019. The second one arose from an invitation to present a talk on my play at an international dance conference in Malaysia and extended my multicultural education. Dance groups from fifteen countries participated, and the performances exhilarated and inspired me creatively. Amidst many workshops, I had the fortune to attend one that was facilitated by the Cambodian Living Arts organization, Cambodia being a country that lost approximately 90 percent of its artists during the Pol Pot regime. While in Malaysia, I availed myself of an opportunity to workshop the play under Director Chin San Sooi using a cast of Malaysian actors. Under his prowess I witnessed new, contrasting character choices. There is something magical about experiencing a director and actors lift your text off the page. It delivers that wonderful aspect of surprise, while resting in the comfort of being a quiet observer, a rather proverbial role for the playwright. Returning to Malaysia allowed me, through another journalist friend, to access the press archives of *The Star*, where I found many articles on the Vietnamese refugees that were absent from the National Archives. I kept photocopies of some prized articles with the hopes that they could be projected or used in some form in the play's production. Maybe someday.

Though essentially a human story, a play about the Vietnamese refugees necessitates a discussion and understanding of the political divisions that are still a matter of reconciliation within the Vietnamese diaspora today. In May of 2019, Eddin Khoo wisely remarked, "How do you put across the human story amidst the great confusion and legitimacy of everyone's grievances?" It was a seed and it reminded me of my father's mantra, "If we understand someone, we don't judge them. And if we judge them, we don't understand them." I realized the play had a representation limited to the refugees, like May's family, who fled Việt Nam, and those they encountered along the way. But what of the people who stayed behind, who believed in communism? Should they be represented? I remembered another of my father's pearls of wisdom, "All sides of a story must be heard." Widening my lens, I decided to expand the character of Smoking Man. Researching the Indigenous H'mong People, I went down another rabbit hole, throwing my energy into a character who would reveal himself, paradoxically, as a communist. And I found his humanity, and came to understand the other side. I consider myself to be neutral in terms of Vietnamese politics, because I was not there. However, everyone is entitled to their own beliefs, and it is also fair that this other side, communism, be represented rather than judged from a distance. I am grateful to those who influenced a deeper investigation because I now feel that the scene with Smoking Man (act 2, scene 5) includes a broader context, and some of my best writing in the play.

As one can imagine, the development of a play takes years of research and time to mull over its themes. That cogitation still happens for me. For example: this play depicts a lot of female relationships, including between mothers and daughters, sisters, female friends and enemies. I have since wondered about the effects of patriarchy on these relationships: If our female relationships were kept intact, how much healthier would our society be?

I don't see *we the same* solely as a political story, though it will carry that tone for some. For many it is a story about refugees, anti-racism, family relationships, othering, survival, finding one's voice, feminism. For me, it is all that and more: *we the same* is an overarching view of humanity, with all of its beauty and ugliness. Each reader will resonate with certain themes, and that is the lure of art.

I envisioned *we the same* as a vehicle for good. It created a platform for Asian Canadian artists to share their stories, to experiment with cultural art forms, and to further learn from each other. Over the years, I homed in on a cast of six Asian Canadian actors, five of whom are Vietnamese Canadian. Upon realizing my original intention of working with an Asian Canadian director could not be fulfilled by the play's producer, I stipulated the creation of an assistant-director mentorship for an Asian Canadian person identifying as female. A conversation with Richard Lee at the Wuchien Michael Than Foundation led to additional funding for this purpose, that is, to influence future diversity in the landscape of Vancouver theatre directors. I devised multiple panels involving speakers from various backgrounds in order to create audience tools and resources. Years of relationship-building and engagement resulted in global collaborations, as well as my bringing nine community partners to the play's production. My friend Amelie Nguyen, of Anh and Chi Vietnamese restaurant, and I came up with a "dinner-and-theatre package," in collaboration with The Cultch, for audiences to enjoy while live-streaming in the comfort of their homes. And finally, while I normally do not publicize my philanthropy, I find it prudent to state my earliest intention to allocate personal profits from the play's premiere production towards related charities, donating 92 percent of my playwright's fee. A preliminary donation went to Ruby Slippers Theatre during the early days of the COVID-19 pandemic. The bulk of donations went to: the Canadian Red Cross's COVID-19 Global Appeal; the Elizabeth F. Precious Endowment, founded by Dalhousie Faculty of Dentistry mentor and world-renowned oral surgeon Dr. David Precious, to treat babies with a cleft lip and palate in Việt Nam; and The Cultch – because theatres, through live storytelling, stimulate visceral experiences and relationships in a way that digital technology cannot. The Cultch supported me unconditionally as an artist, and I don't think I would have survived certain challenges without the support of Heather Redfern and her team. I have eternal gratitude for May, Jean, and their family; Rachel Ditor, my outstanding dramaturge; and Andrew, my rock.

I hope you enjoy reading *we the same.*

With love,

SANGEETA

A NOTE FROM MUSICIAN NGUYỄN HỮU ĐẠT

Sangeeta Wylie and I met through a mutual friend one night at a jazz bar called Sax N' Art, in Hồ Chí Minh City, on April 30, 2019 – an important date in Việt Nam's history.[1] I remember singing "Ain't No Sunshine" by Bill Withers, accompanied by the wonderful saxophonist Trần Mạnh Tuấn. Sangeeta and I became fast friends, later attending a play together and having deep conversations about Vietnamese culture and music. On one of these occasions, I sang, accompanied by my guitar, several songs from various genres and origins. Sangeeta loved the Vietnamese songs, particularly "Ngỡ đâu tình đã quên mình" (I thought love had forgotten me). She expressed the wish that I would one day sing at a future live performance of her play *we the same* in Canada.

But when the day came to fulfill this wish, I couldn't fly over to perform live because of the COVID-19 pandemic. Sangeeta then commissioned me to record a couple of songs from my home in Việt Nam and send them over to Canada, so they could be played during the performance of the play. We talked about the love scene beforehand, and I recorded the song using my intuition about what that scene meant, singing some bars a cappella.

"Ngỡ đâu tình đã quên mình" is a composition by the late Vietnamese musician Lê Hựu Hà. Each sentence in the song's lyrics is very expressive, blending with its surroundings to become a masterpiece in my heart. Whenever I have the chance, I want to sing this song for those who are broken-hearted. Readers or listeners, when you are sitting at home, turn on this song and listen.[2] Hopefully, you will feel like I am sitting next to you and singing to you. Then, one day, we will meet again and have a performance for everyone to come and hear me sing this immortal love song in the flesh.

But for now, we invite you to find yourself a private corner, slow down, and enjoy the love song that is *we the same*.

—HỮU NGUYỄN, 2021

---

1   April 30, 1975, marked the end of the Vietnam War, known in Việt Nam as the American War. On this day, the Việt Cộng captured the city of Sài Gòn. In Việt Nam it has been referred to as the Liberation of Saigon / Reunification Day; in some overseas Vietnamese communities it has been called the Fall of Saigon.

2   On YouTube: Nguyễn Hữu Đạt, "Hữu Nguyễn – Ngỡ Đâu Tình Đã Quên Mình (Acoustic Version)," November 7, 2021, youtu.be/M75nFSANoHk. On SoundCloud: Hữu Nguyễn, "Ngỡ Đâu Tình Đã Quên Mình (Acoustic Version)," November 7, 2021, soundcloud .com/nguyenhuudat1512/ngo-dau-tinh-da-quen-minh-acoustic-version.

we the same

PRODUCTION HISTORY

we the same was first produced by Ruby Slippers Theatre and premiered on November 3, 2021, at The Cultch in Vancouver, British Columbia, with the following cast and crew:

HÀ	Elizabeth Thai
MAI	Grace Le
BẢO and others	Chris Lam
CHINH and others	Brandy Le
CHÂU and others	Quynh Mi
KIM, BIÊN, and others	Khaira Ledeyo

Director:	Diane Brown
Assistant Director:	Patricia Trinh
Cultural Consultants:	Stella Nhung Davis, Tammy Le-Son and Nguyễn Thị Minh Ngọc
Set Designer:	Kimira Reddy
Lighting Designer:	Sophie Tang
Sound Designer:	Matthias Falvai
Visual Designers:	Shanghan Chien, Chimerik Collective
Live Music Composer:	Vi An Diep
Commissioned Musical Recordings:	Nguyễn Hữu Đạt
Choreographer:	Shanny Rann
Costume Designer:	Melicia Zaini
Puppets Creation:	Mark Parlett and Jamie Skidmore
Stage Manager:	Susan D. Currie
Assistant Stage Manager:	Taylor MacKinnon
Dramaturgy:	Rachel Ditor and Amylynn Strilchuk
Projection Designer:	Chimerik 似不像
Lead Designer:	Shang-Han Chien
Animator and Assistant Designer:	Ivan So
New Media Design Advisor and Facilitator:	Sammy Chien
Photographer:	Emily Cooper

CHARACTERS

MAJOR CHARACTERS: Minimum cast of five actors (three women and two men). Two main actors play Mai and Hà, respectively, while three secondary actors play multiple roles.

MAI: Vietnamese Canadian woman, thirty-five years old (but four to five years old in scenes from the past). Mai has been correcting her mother Hà's English since she was young. Though habitual, there are elements of belittling and embarrassment in this dynamic. In Sino-Vietnamese,[1] the name Mai means "plum" or "apricot," or the respective trees that produce them.

HÀ: Vietnamese woman, thirty years old in 1979 (in most scenes), in her sixties in the present (again, throughout the play), and fifteen in 1965 (act 2, scene 2); Mai's mother. Though seemingly simple, Hà is clever, deliberately engaging in word play. Less educated, she seeks Mai's approval. The name means "river" or, metonymically, "water."

BẢO: Thirty-two-year-old Vietnamese man, and Hà's husband. Jovial, outgoing. The actor playing Bảo may also play Huynh, Smoking Man, and Malaysian Officer. The name means "protector."

KIM: Vietnamese female refugee, twenty-four years old. Kind, educated, outspoken. The actor playing Kim may also play Châu, Linh, Biên, and Tiên. The name means "metal" or "gold."

BIÊN: Vietnamese female refugee and sex worker in her early thirties. Cunning. The actor playing Biên may also play Vietnamese Woman, Châu, Kim, Linh, and Tiên. The name means "frontier, boundary."

MINOR CHARACTERS: Minor roles can be doubled up with other roles.

CHÂU: Hà's twenty-four-year-old sister, also called Auntie Six. Born in Việt Nam. The actor playing Châu may also play Vietnamese Woman, Kim, Linh, Biên, Tiên, and Visa Officer. The name means "gem" or "pearl."

LINH: Hà and Bảo's eight-year-old daughter. Nurturing. The actor playing Linh may also play Vietnamese Woman, Châu, Kim, Biên, and Tiên. The name means "spirit, soul."

---

1   Sino-Vietnamese is words and characters in the Vietnamese language that have historically been borrowed from the Chinese language.

CHINH: Hà and Bảo's seven-year-old son. He feels like an outcast. The actor playing Chinh may also play Vietnamese Man, Biên's Husband, Captain, Mr. Long. The name means "orderly, righteous."

MR. LONG: Vietnamese man, thirty-five years old in 1965 (act 2, scene 2) and fifty years old in 1979 (act 2, scene 8). Owner of a textile factory. The actor playing Mr. Long may also play Vietnamese Man, Chinh, Biên's Husband, and Captain. The name means "dragon."

SMOKING MAN: Poet and Việt Cộng of H'Mông origin,[2] thirty-ish but looking much older, hardened by life.

HUYNH: Hà and Bảo's six-year-old son. The actor playing Huynh may also play Bảo, Smoking Man, and Malaysian Officer. The name means "yellow, gold-coloured."

VIETNAMESE MAN
VIETNAMESE WOMAN
MOTHER
MALAYSIAN GUARD
TIÊN
BIÊN'S HUSBAND
MÁ
CAPTAIN
MUSLIM WOMAN
VISA OFFICER

Non-Speaking Characters

OLD MALAYSIAN MAN
REFUGEE MAN
REFUGEE WOMAN
SECURITY
HẠNH (two-year-old daughter of Hà and Bảo)
NIEN (one-year-old son of Hà and Bảo)
SHADOWY WOMAN

---

2   The H'Mông are an Indigenous People from southwest China and southeast Asia.

NOTES ON PERFORMANCE

we the same is a universal story of humanity, not a political commentary or tool. The association of political symbols like Vietnamese flags in promotional material (posters, advertising) for the staging of the play is discouraged, as it goes against the play's meaning and intention.

About dialects: In the **present**, Hà speaks with broken English and a Vietnamese accent. In the opening scene, Vietnamese Man and Vietnamese Women step into the present and speak with Vietnamese accents. In the **past**, it is understood that the characters are speaking in Vietnamese or in their native tongues, and therefore no accents are used.

Casting suggestion: Younger children, Nien and Hạnh, may be imagined or inanimate (puppets carried by Hà or Linh, for example).

Staging suggestion: Shadow play or puppetry can depict mythological creatures (for example, Lạc Long, Âu Cơ) and the fifty men in Pulau Aur.

Musical suggestions: "Gia tài của mẹ" (My mother's legacy), composed and sung by Trịnh Công Sơn. Currently banned in Việt Nam. See, for example, youtu.be/8sFOmBDl8lY.
"Ngỡ đâu tình đã quên mình" (I thought love had forgotten me), composed by Lê Hựu Hà and sung by Nguyễn Hữu Đạt.[3] youtu .be/M75nFSANoHk or soundcloud.com/nguyenhuudat1512 /ngo-dau-tinh-da-quen-minh-acoustic-version.
"Trả lại em yêu" (Return, my love), composed by Phạm Duy and sung by Lệ Thu. youtu.be/WME5XNU5eEI or mtqmusic.bandcamp.com/track /tr-l-i-em-y-u.
"Biển nhớ" (Sea of remembrance), composed by Trịnh Công Sơn and sung by Khánh Ly. Played when the Vietnamese left the refugee camps and therefore resonant for many today. youtu.be/CowW8pRypHc.
"Hello Vietnam," English adaptation by Guy Balbaert of "Bonjour Vietnam," composed by Marc Lavoine and Yvan Coriat and recorded by the Vietnamese Belgian singer Pham Quỳnh Anh. youtu.be/VGRc-cIoJbA.

Act 1, scene 1; act 2, scene 10: The bamboo sticks referred to in these scenes, known as "kau chim" or "kau cim" (Chinese fortune sticks), are

---

3 See "A Note from Musician Nguyễn Hữu Đạt."

used by the Vietnamese in fortune telling. Sticks are numbered to match scrolls written in Chinese characters. A Buddhist monk translates the scroll. Both references (in the prologue of act 1 and the audio track of act 2) should be staged.

Act 1, scene 3: "You remember the pig?": A living pig should not be used in this scene. One may use audio to imply the presence of the animal.

Act 1, scene 4; act 2, scene 3: The hooting isn't produced by a literal owl but is used symbolically. In Vietnamese culture, an owl hoot is regarded as an omen of death or illness.

Act 1, scene 5: "*They freeze while pirates ... violently mirror the children's play*": A Vietnamese martial art (for example, Vovinam) may be used to represent pirate action in the background. Vovinam, short for Võ Việt Nam and officially known as Việt Võ Đạo, translates as "Vietnamese Martial Arts."

Act 1, scene 7: "*MALAYSIAN GUARD guides the refugees*": At the time, Malaysia had a policy to turn back Vietnamese refugees, resulting in refugee boats being towed back to the sea. Malaysian Deputy Prime Minister Mahathir Mohamad was quoted by news outlets in June 1979 saying the refugees should be "shot on sight." Responding to the United Nations Secretary-General Kurt Waldheim's request for explanation, Mohamad wouldn't unequivocally withdraw his statement: "We've already been accused by *Newsweek* of shooting illegal immigrants, so we might as well do it and justify their accusation." Amid world outrage, Malaysian government officials later stated Mohamad had been misquoted and had in fact said that the Malaysian police force should "shoo" the refugees, not "shoot" them.[4]

---

4   See, for example: Henry Kamm, "Malaysia Cancels Threats to Refugees," *New York Times*, June 19, 1979, A3, www.nytimes.com/1979/06/19/archives/malaysia-cancels-threats-to-refugees-the-goal-of-the-comments.html; Jana K. Lipman, "To 'Shoot' or to 'Shoo': Vietnamese in Malaysia, 1975–1979," in *In Camps: Vietnamese Refugees, Asylum Seekers, and Repatriates* (Berkeley: University of California Press, 2020), 52–89, doi.org/10.1525/9780520975064-003; and Frankie D'Cruz, "When Dr M's 'Shoot' Became 'Shoo' – and Story On Boat People Got Shot Down," Free Malaysia Today (FMT), February 5, 2022, www.freemalaysiatoday.com/category/nation/2022/02/05/when-dr-ms-shoot-became-shoo-and-story-on-boat-people-got-shot-down/.

Act 1, scene 8: Kim's description of her father's "trees [being] black," their "fruit withered to nothing," is a reference to the use by the US military of the lethal herbicide nicknamed Agent Orange (actually a mix of two herbicides, 2,4-dichlorophenoxyacetic acid and 2,4,5-trichlorophenoxyacetic acid) during the Vietnam War as a weapon and defoliant.

Act 1, scene 10: "*A Cham ritual dance* ... The whales guided our boat": The Cham people of Champa, now inhabiting central and southern Việt Nam, are pre-Vietnamese (second century to 1832). They are of Sanskrit origins and Hindu, Buddhist, and Islamic faiths. Cham fishers performed a ritual dance to Shiva, God of whales, in a bid to procure divine protection by invoking the help of whales during ocean storms.

Act 2, scene 2: "*BẢO is dipping spools of thread into dye*": The spools of thread are the size of paper-towel rolls. They are dipped in dye and then tossed to the lower floor for the workers to gather and box.

Act 2, scene 4: "That's not rice wine": Known in southern Vietnam as rượu đế, which translates as "state-slip-away liquor" (to distinguish it from "state-enterprise liquor"), it was distilled in secret during the French imperialist government's monopoly on alcohol production. Vietnamese rice wine, sometimes referred to as contraband liquor, is traditionally made at home, cheap, ubiquitous, and potent.

During the party, Hà says, "Death is just a word that belongs in the past or the future." This is a play on a few things:
1. Zen Buddhist philosophy, which teaches that death is a phase or period unto itself, with its own past and future;
2. the word *death* as it temporally relates to "dying" (sometime in the future) or "having died" (sometime in the past), but not "being dead" (in the present). In other words, it *happened* or *will happen* but is not *happening*;
3. the qualities of the Vietnamese language, which does not conjugate verbs. Often, Vietnamese relies on context for temporal indications. Past and future tenses can be conveyed by prefixing verbs with particles đã and sẽ, respectively. Later in the scene, Kim says, "It's always present," thereby reflecting on how Vietnamese verbs somehow always denote the present tense.

Act 2, scene 5: "One who drinks will drink again" and "When the tree is fallen, everyone runs to it with their axe" are old Vietnamese proverbs, author unknown.

Mersing, Malaysia: A small coastal town in Malaysia where many Vietnamese refugee boats landed at the time. Once there, their passengers were mostly transferred by Malaysian police to an enclosed soccer field where they awaited their fate.

"Every night I see them. Butterflies": In Vietnamese culture, the butterfly symbolizes the soul, reincarnation, resurrection, and femininity. In this reference, butterflies are made to represent the souls of dead soldiers.

"Diệm put Catholics in the Highlands": Ngô Đình Diệm (1901–1963) was the last prime minister of the State of Vietnam and the first president of South Vietnam, until his assassination in 1963 during a US-backed coup d'état. The violence and repression that characterized Diệm's reign culminated in the Buddhist crisis (Biến cố Phật giáo) of 1963 and the self-immolation of monk Thích Quảng Đức, memorialized in a famous photograph by Malcolm Brown.

Act 2, scene 7: An "orang bunian" is a benevolent supernatural being from Malaysian folklore. Orang bunian literally translates to "hidden people" or "whistling people"; they are only visible to those with 'spiritual sight'." For further reference, see mythlok.com/orang-bunian/.

Act 2, scene 8: "Sister Monica runs our transit camp there": Sister Monica was the Mother Superior in charge of the Infant Jesus Sisters Convent in Cheras, Kuala Lumpur. Under Sister Monica's partial supervision, and in spite of her lack of official connection, the Malaysian Red Crescent Society was able to establish a transit camp, known as Canada Camp, for refugees selected for immigration to Canada. It was an unexpectedly successful operation. I visited this convent in 2019 and interviewed one of two surviving nuns, Sister Agnes, about her memories of that time. Sister Monica's name came up several times during my interviews, including with Canadian visa officers, who spoke fondly of her.

ACT 1

SCENE 1

PROLOGUE

The streets of Sài Gòn, 1979. Vendors squatting, selling noodles, fruit, and rice. They are gossiping. Cyclos ("xích lô") and bicycles roll through. A man dressed in jeans, wearing a conical bamboo hat, plays the folk song "Gia tài của mẹ" (My mother's legacy) by Trịnh Công Sơn on the đàn ghi ta, the Vietnamese guitar. A sex worker keeps watch for customers. HÀ, a thirty-year-old Vietnamese woman, enters an open-air Buddhist temple. She picks up a wooden cylinder containing long bamboo sticks and shakes it.[5] A Công An, or neighbourhood police officer, enters. The music stops; the people in the street disperse.

Lights fade.

Present day. Spotlight on VIETNAMESE MAN, stepping out of the street scene.

VIETNAMESE MAN: I leave in 1978 by boat. We get attack by pirate. Every twenty minute.

A second spotlight comes up on VIETNAMESE WOMAN, stepping out of the street scene.

VIETNAMESE WOMAN: We try to leave many time. One time my parent get arrest. Throw in jail.

VIETNAMESE MAN: We refuse to back down. One pirate attack one end, another attack the other end.

VIETNAMESE WOMAN: In 1979 I leave with my aunt uncle. We try go south. To Malaysia or Indonesia.

VIETNAMESE MAN: My boat is cut on both end, and we start to sink. People hold on in the water. All night.

---

5   See Notes on Performance.

11

VIETNAMESE WOMAN: No Singapore. They not take anyone. But there is storm, it blow us away.

Fade to black.

Spotlights on two Vietnamese women, MAI and HÀ, both in their early thirties. They speak directly to the audience. It is later revealed that MAI is recording herself. HÀ, overhearing MAI, relives the 1979 memory depicted in act 2, scene 8, in which she's speaking to a VISA OFFICER. (There may be a staged memory effect for HÀ – sound, light, a sense of being underwater, etc.)

MAI: We left Việt Nam when I was four.

HÀ: I'm thirty. I was twenty-nine when we left.

MAI: I was five when we got to Canada. A year later.

HÀ: We left in May.

MAI: Six of us under the age of eight.

HÀ: I have six children. We're on our own.

MAI: Two months on the sea, with typhoons and pirate attacks. We nearly starved to death. I don't remember anything.

HÀ: We got separated in Malaysia.

MAI: My first memory is being hit by a car, in Victoria. I was five. We left Việt Nam because we were poor.

HÀ, snapped out of her memory, is now in her sixties. Lights reveal MAI's present home.

HÀ: No. We not poor then. We poor during the war. And we poor in Canada. But not when we leave.

MAI turns to HÀ.

MAI: I thought we couldn't buy rice?

HÀ: We not buy rice because we rich.

MAI: That makes no sense.

HÀ: (*noticing MAI's recording*) Who you talk to?

MAI: It's a recording for Jadyn's project.

HÀ: Why *you* do it?

MAI: Because. She needs my help.

HÀ tsks disapprovingly.

HÀ: Jadyn can do her own work.

MAI ignores her mother's dig.

MAI: The internet's a jungle. It's my job to weed it.

HÀ: You never ask me.

MAI: You said you didn't want to talk about it –

HÀ: I don't.

MAI: – that you can't remember everything –

HÀ: Yes.

MAI: Then why are you upset?

Beat.

HÀ: What you tell Jadyn?

MAI: She wants to know about Việt Nam. She's the only one in her class who doesn't know her roots. She feels left out.

HÀ: Teach her cook Vietnamese food.

MAI: Mom, I don't cook Vietnamese food.

HÀ: Why?

MAI: Because. You never taught me.

HÀ: I busy, with six kid. But now you learn from computer everything –
from Goog Le.

MAI: Google.

*HÀ takes the correction in stride, biting her tongue: MAI has
been correcting her mother's English since she was young.*

HÀ: You want I teach you?

MAI: (*edgy*) I don't need you to teach me, Mom. Jadyn's your
granddaughter. Don't you want her to know about her family?

*HÀ is torn between keeping her secrets of the past buried and
wanting what's best for her granddaughter.*

HÀ: (*conceding*) Okay. I tell Jadyn. Later. When she older.

MAI: (*dismissively*) Yeah, right.

HÀ: What that mean?

MAI: Nothing. You never took us to Việt Nam.

HÀ: Mai. Việt Nam not the same. It in the past. Why go back?

MAI: Maybe because I feel like I have no past –

HÀ: That not true –

MAI: – or I feel like it's been made up. I can't tell what's real
and what's not.

HÀ: What not real?

MAI: You said in Sài Gòn we lived in a two-bedroom house. All of us in one bedroom, and Grandma and Granddad in the other.

HÀ: That the way in Việt Nam. You Canadian. You need big home, too many room.

MAI: Eight people in one bedroom is not rich. Even by Vietnamese standards.

HÀ: Seven.

HÀ realizes her mistake too late.

MAI: Seven? There were eight of us!

HÀ: No.

MAI: What are you saying? Everyone was born when we left. Nien was one. You're mixed up –

HÀ: No, you mix up! We only seven then!

MAI: Dad?

HÀ: Your father there!

MAI: Then who was missing?!

Transition to the next scene: HÀ and MAI travel back to 1979, where they begin to see the family's story unfold – a story which they follow together until their ultimate return to the present in act 2, scene 10. NB: The action is continuous in the past, even when the characters speak from the present.

SCENE 2

SÀI GÒN

Sài Gòn, late afternoon. A modest kitchen. On a low table there are dishes with food untouched. A bucket of charcoal in one corner. In another corner is an altar for honouring the ancestors. HÀ holds sticks of lit incense between her palms and bows to the altar. As CHÂU enters, she chants a mantra, for example "Namu Myōhō Renge Kyō" (Glory to the Dharma of the Lotus Sūtra).

CHÂU: Where's Bảo?

HÀ places the incense on the altar, picks up a dish, and moves to the kitchen.

HÀ: He's gone to buy rice.

CHÂU: Black market?

HÀ shushes her: the walls have ears.

CHÂU: I came to talk to you about Chinh.

HÀ: Bring me the dishes.

CHÂU gathers a dish from the table and returns to HÀ, who consolidates the food into one dish.

HÀ: Were you teaching today?

CHÂU: Yes. I finished the "special courses."[6]

HÀ: They're still firing teachers?

---

6   In 1979 the Vietnamese government imposed the third educational reform: a new twelve-year general education system, including new textbooks and revised social sciences courses, replacing South Vietnamese teachers with officials from the North, and mandatory retraining courses for teachers.

CHÂU: Thirty days of re-education camp[7] – they don't come back. They say the Hoa[8] can return to China. But in the north, the Red River is full of Chinese blood.

HÀ: China has left Việt Nam. It should be better for us now.

CHÂU: It was more peaceful when we were at war. Việt Nam wants to be Vietnamese again. No Americans, French, Japanese, or Chinese. No foreigners. No opposition! They found out about Hạnh's husband: came at midnight and took them away.

Beat.

CHÂU: You were blessed that Bảo never fought –

HÀ: If we were blessed, Chinh would not be living with you.

CHÂU: The war is over. You sell so many pens, they say Bảo is the ink man. You must have money now.

HÀ: What money we have is no good. We can't buy rice.

Beat.

CHÂU: Let me bring Chinh back to you.

HÀ: He's safer with you.

CHÂU: The war is over now.

HÀ: It's not my place.

CHÂU: You are his mother.

---

7   Hundreds of thousands of South Vietnamese were imprisoned in "re-education camps" for the purpose of indoctrination and to punish "war criminals." Terms ranged from weeks to years, and torture was common.

8   Vietnamese citizens of Han Chinese ancestry.

17

HÀ: They are my husband's parents. I can't disrespect them. Just as I'm your older sister and you shouldn't disrespect me.

CHÂU: I'm only thinking of you. And your son. Chị.[9] If you're hiding anything –

HÀ: We're not hiding anything, em.[10]

BẢO enters, out of breath and agitated.

BẢO: Hà! Oh! Hello, Châu. Khỏe không?[11]

CHÂU: Dạ khỏe, anh Bảo.[12]

CHÂU bows her head. HÀ puts a finger to her lips.

HÀ: Your parents are taking a nap. Everyone has eaten.

BẢO: Sorry –

HÀ: Where's the rice?

BẢO shakes his head.

HÀ: Eat. Try again tomorrow.

BẢO: No. It's not safe.

CHÂU: What happened?

BẢO: I was followed.

HÀ: Who?

---

9   Older sister.

10 Younger sibling or a term of endearment.

11 How are you?

12 Fine, brother Bảo.

BẢO: The Công an.[13]

CHÂU: Why would he follow you?

BẢO: I don't know.

CHÂU: This is what I'm talking about. No one's safe anymore –

BẢO: Châu –

CHÂU: People are leaving! Chị! You need to think of your children –

BẢO: Châu! We cannot leave. Go home now. I need to talk to my wife alone.

CHÂU: Chào, anh chị.[14]

CHÂU exits.

HÀ: Don't worry about the rice. We've two cassava roots.

BẢO: Hà. They know.

HÀ: What are you saying –

BẢO: No one would sell me rice. We've been blacklisted – the Công An knows we have money!

HÀ: Did you give him the gold?

BẢO: (*shaking his head angrily*) They've taken enough of my money!

HÀ: Châu's right! No one's safe anymore!

BẢO: Why was Châu here?

---

13 The Vietnam People's Public Security (Công an Nhân dân Việt Nam), the neighbourhood spying police.

14 See you later, brother and sister.

HÀ: She wants to bring Chinh back.

BẢO: Ba Má[15] won't allow it.

HÀ: The war's over now!

BẢO: Not in Cambodia! Hà. The only way is to leave.

HÀ: You just told Châu we can't leave –

BẢO: We can. But Châu can't know our plans.

HÀ: What plans? You want to leave by boat? People are dying on the sea. And on the shore – they're bombing the boats!

BẢO: Either we die on the sea, or I die in Cambodia. We don't have a choice! I won't let them dump us in the jungle![16]

HÀ: Châu says you can't trust the boat captains –

BẢO: Who can we trust? First, they took our money. They said we should be grateful to have food. Then they took our rice. They said we should be grateful to have religion. Then they tried to take our Gods. But God left Việt Nam a long time ago! It's time we follow.

HÀ: It's too dangerous! Your parents won't survive –

BẢO: Ba Má aren't coming.

HÀ: We can't leave them behind! What will happen to them when the cộng sản[17] come?

---

15 Father and Mother.

16 Between 1975 and 1980, the Vietnamese communist government implemented the New Economic Zones program, confiscating properties of Southern Vietnamese and forcibly relocating them to labour camps to establish new agriculture in uninhabited forested areas. Most were city dwellers who lacked farming skills. Conditions were poor, with reports of starvation, disease, and death.

17 The communists.

BẢO: They won't leave Việt Nam. Brother Four will look after them. We can live without Ba Má, but no Vietnamese can live without loyal neighbours. They're all turning, one by one.

HÀ: What about Chinh?

BẢO: Tell Châu we'll take him back. But don't tell her why. No one can know. Not even family.

Beat.

Every morning I wake with Fear in my stomach. We can't even buy rice without being followed! Hà. I feel like I'm suffocating.

HÀ: Aren't you afraid of drowning in the ocean?

BẢO: I'd rather die at sea than at the hand of a Communist –

HÀ: Ssh!

BẢO: (*attempting to tease her*) At least on the sea, we won't die *right* away.

HÀ smiles in spite of herself: it's their inside joke.

HÀ: (*conceding*) I'll start packing.

BẢO: No. We bring nothing. Only what we wear. A little food. Milk for the baby. Everything else, we leave behind.

HÀ grabs a handful of gold bars, through the bucket of charcoal.

HÀ: What about our gold?

BẢO: Sew it into my shirt. I'll carry what I can. The rest remains hidden, for Ba Má. After we're gone, the ancestors will guide them.

HÀ: If you're caught with the gold –

BẢO: If I'm caught, it's only me.

The scene switches to the present.

MAI: I don't understand. Chinh was living with Auntie Six?

HÀ: It a long time ago, before you were born.

MAI: Why?

HÀ: Many time you are look after, too. Your grandma and aunties look
after all five of you. That normal.

MAI: That's not the same. Why wasn't Chinh living with us?

HÀ: He live with Auntie Six for a few year.

MAI: How many years?

HÀ: Five year.

MAI: Five years! He was ... two –

HÀ: He seven, when we leave.

MAI: And we grabbed him and left? Chinh must've been confused –

HÀ: No time. We leave fast. In secret –

SCENE 3

LEAVING

HÀ continues speaking to MAI without missing a beat. The sound of ocean waves crashing on a beach melts into the sound of pouring rain.

HÀ: The day we leave, is pouring rain. We walk, so we don't draw any attention. I carry Hạnh and Nien, your father carry food and milk. The rest of you hold hand so you do not fall. A mile from home, we meet Mr. Lê, a farmer with old truck. We sit in the back. With a pig. I wish we go fast, but many bicycle, car, and animal, everywhere. Car stuck in the mud and the ditch. One bus fall down. It go on fire, become burning coffin. Seem like everyone try to leave Việt Nam one way or another.

MAI: I remember. I was scared of the pig.

HÀ: You remember the pig?

MAI: We were pretty crammed in there.

HÀ: Do you remember what happened to the pig?

MAI is transported back to 1979. The family is in the bed of a farmer's truck, being driven out of Sài Gòn. Everyone is asleep except for MAI and CHINH, who is playing with rubber bands.[18]

MAI: Chinh, where did you find the rubber bands?

CHINH: Má – Auntie Six gave them to me.

MAI: How do you play?

---

18 There are several traditional Vietnamese childrens' games that employ rubber bands. Chơi búng thun, or snap elastic, involves using a single finger to jump your rubber band onto an opponent's. See specialkid.vn/blogs/cac-tro-choi-cho-be/tro-choi-dan-gian-bung-chun.

CHINH: I'll show you. First you have to touch the pig.

MAI: No.

CHINH: What's wrong?

MAI: Nothing.

CHINH: Then touch the pig.

MAI: You do it first.

CHINH: It's easy. Watch.

> *CHINH pats the pig.*

CHINH: See? Your turn. Give me your hand.

> *MAI holds her hand out. CHINH uses MAI's hand to pull the pig's tail. It grunts and squeals.*

MAI: Stop, Chinh!

CHINH: What a baby! Mai is scared of a pig!

MAI: That's not fair!

BẢO: Children! We have to be quiet. Stop crying, Mai. It's only a pig. He's more scared of you.

MAI: What if he bites me?

BẢO: (*teasingly*) Mai, you won't die *right* away. Now apologize to each other.

MAI: Chinh started it ...

BẢO: Mai, he is anh Chinh.[19] You must respect your older brother.

---

19 Older brother Chinh.

MAI: But Ba –

BẢO: No back talk. Children. Say sorry.

MAI: I'm sorry, anh.

CHINH: I'm sorry, em.

BẢO nods his head approvingly, takes a beat, then deliberately switches to a mythological story.

BẢO: Mm-hmm. The Mekong has nine rivers, named for dragons. One of Việt Nam's ancient kings was named Lạc Long Quân. Lạc Long ruled over the land near the sea. He wanted to live underwater, so he turned into a dragon. When his people needed their king, they would call upon him and he would come back to the land.

Lạc Long fell in love with a beautiful mountain fairy named Âu Cơ. They married, and she gave birth to a pouch filled with one hundred eggs. After seven days, each egg hatched into a child.

Though Lạc Long and Âu Cơ were deeply in love, they came from different worlds. Lạc Long missed the sea, and Âu Cơ missed the mountains. They separated, each taking fifty children, and promised to help each other when needed. The children became the rulers of the Hundred Việt, the tribes of Việt Nam, that still exist today. No matter where you are, Vietnamese always keep this promise to love and protect one another.

It's time to rest, children. When you wake up, we'll be in the Mekong.

BẢO closes his eyes. MAI makes sure he's asleep.

MAI: Anh Chinh!

CHINH: What?

MAI: Where are your rubber bands?

CHINH: Why?

MAI: I need them. For the pig.

CHINH: I thought you were afraid of the pig.

MAI: Ba says the pig is afraid. Like Lạc Long's people. We have to set him free.

> *LINH wakes up. CHINH and MAI are tying rubber bands together.*

LINH: What are you doing?

CHINH: Mai wants to set the pig free.

LINH: How?

MAI: Tie his mouth with rubber bands, so he can't bite.

CHINH: And then what?

MAI: I'll push him so he can jump off. Linh, you can help us.

LINH: I don't think this is a good idea.

CHINH: I'll do the rubber bands, and you lift Mai.

LINH: I'm not helping you. Ba wouldn't like it. I don't think you should do it.

CHINH: It's just a pig. Fine. I'll lift Mai.

> *CHINH helps MAI climb onto the edge of the truck. CHINH tries to put the rubber bands around the pig's snout. The pig squeals. BẢO wakes up to see MAI fall onto the pig. The pig bucks MAI off and jumps off the truck, running away. The truck stops.*

BẢO: Children! What have you done!

CHINH: Nothing, Ba.

BẢO: Nothing? The pig has run off. What did you do?

MAI: We were helping, like Lạc Long –

BẢO: Linh, you've disappointed me. You're supposed to take care of your brothers and sisters.

LINH: I tried to stop them, Ba. They wouldn't listen to me –

CHINH: It was Mai's idea –

MAI: We wanted to help, like the dragon, Ba. The pig was –

BẢO: Quiet. Look what you've done! We don't have extra money to pay for a pig. Mai. Come here.

The scene switches to the present.

MAI: He was so angry, he gave me a spanking. I was the only one who got punished. I could've really hurt myself.

HÀ: You okay.

MAI: I bumped my head. I could've had a concussion.

HÀ: Children bump their head all the time.

The scene switches to the past.

BẢO: Children stay here while we get the pig.

BẢO exits the truck and walks towards the pig, who is grazing on the roadside. HÀ speaks from the present while a loud bang cracks through the air. The pig runs away.

HÀ: A few minute after we stop, a bomb go off. Then quiet. Metal, clothing, body part everywhere. Land in river, too. The bridge we need to take is gone.

MAI: We were lucky.

27

HÀ: Not lucky. Mr. Lê want more money. For the pig. For the long drive. We give him more gold.

MAI: We would've been blown apart, if we hadn't stopped. He should have been grateful!

HÀ: This Việt Nam. Everyone want gold. Only thing that keep secret.

MAI: It's backwards.

HÀ: (*wittingly*) Backward, yes. We go backward through the jungle, the long way. More dangerous. Twelve hour to reach Bạc Liêu. All of you tired, hungry, cranky. But the boat captain not here. Forty-five gold bar we pay to Mr. Lê, the boat captain, the dockmaster, city hall, the Công An.

MAI: You had to pay them all?

HÀ: Anyone can report us. The dockmaster: he an old man, could use the money. Or the boat captain. Maybe he not a captain.

MAI: Everyone's lying or bribing each other. How do they sleep at night?

HÀ: We sleep in small shed, on top of each other. Every day we ask, "When the boat is coming?" Not today, not today. More and more people arrive. No place to sleep. After twenty day the boat captain come. Everyone push, shove, use elbow to get in front. No one care about the children: they almost step on you! I have to pick you up quick. I think we not make it. But on June 12, 1979: we get on a boat. It eighteen metric: suppose to hold thirty people. There are over three hundred of us.

SCENE 4

FALSE START

A few hours after the boat has embarked. HÀ, BẢO, and their children, MAI, LINH, CHINH, HUYNH, HẠNH, and NIEN, are on the bottom floor of a crowded boat. There are no windows. They're being pushed, the children cry and gasp for air. BẢO lifts MAI high above his head and notices she can breathe easier. He puts MAI down.

BẢO: Hạnh, come.

BẢO lifts up two-year-old HẠNH. He continues to lift each child one at a time. The movement is fluid, as the boat sways underneath them. The sounds of the children gulping air are layered with the ocean waves. The boat suddenly jerks to a stop, and everyone holds their breath. BẢO nearly drops CHINH, then puts him down. The scene switches to the present.

HÀ: After a few hour, Coast Guard stop us. Near a lighthouse. They make us get off, leave everything on the boat. It dark. Nothing here. No one know if we disappear.

The scene switches to the past. MOTHER enters with her sick, crying baby.

MOTHER: Chị. Do you have any medicine?

HÀ: What's wrong with her?

MOTHER: She's seasick.

HÀ removes medicine from her pocket.

HÀ: Take this.

MOTHER: Thank you, chị.

29

MOTHER bows her head and exits.

HÀ: Why aren't they sending us back?

BẢO: They're checking the boat.

HÀ: For a bomb?

BẢO shrugs. The scene switches to the present.

MAI: Weren't they supposed to arrest you?

HÀ: We think that. But they let us go.

MAI: Why would they do that? Wouldn't the Coast Guard send people back?

HÀ: Wait. Listen to story.

> *The scene switches to the past. BẢO and HÀ enter the boat. The place is ransacked: bags opened and items scattered.*

BẢO: Damn thieves!

HÀ: They've stolen everything! Bảo, we have to go back!

BẢO points to his shirt.

BẢO: They didn't get the gold. We're not going back! They've destroyed what was left of our country! South Việt Nam is dead.

> *BẢO exits in anger. The scene switches to the present.*

HÀ: Your father very angry.

> *MAI, as her older self, comforts HÀ in a silent gesture, for example by helping her tidy the mess.*

HÀ: Finally, we leave Việt Nam again. The sea start to get wavy (*gesturing with her hand*), like that. Old people can not get up.

We have to carry them. The children are throwing up, like the little baby I meet on the beach. The mother keep give her more medicine. But the baby not get better.

MOTHER enters, rocking her baby. We hear an owl hooting, and then the only sound is the ocean rolling its waves, as the water turns angrier. The baby is quiet and still. MOTHER tries to wake her baby, first pinching, then slapping her gently on the cheeks. MOTHER becomes hysterical. She slaps the baby on the back, shakes her. MOTHER sobs, clasping her baby tight, kissing her. She finally holds her baby's lifeless body out to HÀ.

HÀ: She cannot do it. So I take her baby. I hold her over the railing. And I let her go. Into the black water. The sea take her quick, no sound.

MOTHER crumples over in agony and exits.

HÀ: I try to comfort the woman. But there no comfort.

The scene switches to the past.

HÀ: (*to herself*) She gave her too much medicine. Too much medicine.

MAI: Má?

HÀ turns to young MAI and squeezes her tight.

The scene switches to the present. MAI steps out of her mother's embrace.

MAI: It was the first time you ever hugged me.

SCENE 5

PIRATE GAMES

The boat has picked up speed. The sound of roaring engines becomes louder. HÀ speaks from the present during this scene.

HÀ: On the second day, we meet pirate from Thailand. Ten men. With big knife. I swallow my wedding ring before they see. They keep us for hours, cut our water bottle. For many year, Vietnamese fight in jungle. Never give up, fight to the death. But we the one who did not fight. Pirate want our jewellery and gold. We give it all. But not my ring, not the gold we wear.

One young girl very pretty, about sixteen. They rape her.

The scene switches to the past. Spotlight on MAI and CHINH, engrossed in a pirate game.

MAI: I wanna be the pirate now, anh Chinh!

CHINH: Girls can't be pirates!

A struggle ensues between CHINH and MAI. They freeze while pirates (who could be indicated by shadows) violently mirror the children's play (choreographed as a martial art scene, a Vovinam sequence, for example).

HÀ: They go for another girl.

Muted screams of other refugees. The children resume.

MAI: I hate you! You're not my brother. I wish you'd stayed with Auntie Six!

CHINH: I wanna go home!

CHINH exits. The scene switches to the present.

MAI: Oh my god. I was so cruel.

HÀ: You children.

MAI: He was feeling left out. I made it worse.

HÀ: Children say thing they not mean.

MAI: Did we watch that girl get raped?

HÀ: Everyone see.

MAI: We were kids. How could you let us watch that?

HÀ: No place to go. Some boat twenty-two attack. People die, many rape. They throw them on the sea. Some women they take and put in brothel. We lucky. Only one rape.

BEACH SURVIVAL

HÀ continues speaking from the present without missing a beat. Optional prologue to this scene: adding to the sound of ocean waves crashing in previous scenes, an image of a stark-white sand beach is revealed.

HÀ: Two day later we see land. Malaysia. We happy. But the local throw rock at us. They tip the boats, with people on them. The Malaysian send guard. We not allow to leave the beach.

The scene switches to the past. HÀ counts her children like a mother hen. A sixteen-year-old refugee girl, TIÊN, enters. She tentatively approaches MALAYSIAN GUARD in military uniform.

TIÊN: Hello, officer. I'm Tiên. Nice uniform. Must be hard work, guarding us. *(touching him nervously)* You want a special massage?

Young MAI watches as TIÊN holds her fingers up, signifying the price to be with her. HÀ slowly crouches in the water, with MAI at her side.

MAI: Má, can I play with Tiên?

HÀ: Stay away from her, Mai. She's the one the pirates hurt.

MAI: Why?

HÀ: *(deflecting)* Stay here. Tell me if the guard turns around.

TIÊN holds her hand out, pocketing the guard's money under her bra, and exits with her customer. HÀ retrieves her ring in her feces. She uses her shirt and ocean water to scrub the ring. HÀ withdraws from the water, stealing a glance at TIÊN (now offstage).

*BIÊN and BIÊN'S HUSBAND enter. BIÊN kicks sand
in HÀ's face.*

BIÊN: Washerwoman! You were staring at my daughter. You like her? It's
okay, but that'll cost extra for your kind.

HÀ: Mai, come.

BIÊN: You think you're better than me? I saw you digging in your shit.
You think you're so clean?! Here. Wash this!

> *BIÊN starts to take off her dirty shirt. BIÊN'S HUSBAND holds
> his hand out to stop her.*

BIÊN'S HUSBAND: Biên. Leave her alone.

BIÊN: (*mockingly*) Oh, you like her? You wanna fuck her?

BIÊN'S HUSBAND: Shut up.

BIÊN: You shut up, you cocksucker. You're no good to me. At least Tiên
makes money for us. You like this whore, go on. Go have sex. Make
sure she pays you first.

> *BIÊN and BIÊN'S HUSBAND exit, arguing. Young MAI looks
> at her mother.*

MAI: What's sex?

> *Beat.*

HÀ: (*still in the past*) When times are hard, some good people become
bad. And some bad people become very bad.

MAI: Is Tiên bad, Má?

HÀ: Not everyone is who they say they are. (*speaking from the present*)
The face come off, you see the people different. The guard take turn
with Tiên and the other young girls. They do not care who see.

We stay far away. Try to find shelter. The rain come quick. From the side. It very heavy, blow the sand –

MAI closes her eyes.

MAI: (*speaking from the present*) The sand – it was everywhere ... in our eyes, our ears, our mouths. We couldn't see anything. It was hard to breathe.

BẢO and CHINH enter and join young MAI. They sit on the ground and huddle to protect themselves from the sand and rainstorms. CHINH pulls MAI's hair.

MAI: Ow! Stop it, anh Chinh!

BẢO puts his hand out to stop MAI from pushing CHINH.

BẢO: Mai. No.

MAI: He did it first, Ba! He's a monster!

BẢO: Quiet. Girls don't fight with their brothers, even if they're monsters.

CHINH: I'm not a monster! I wanna go home.

BẢO: We have no home, Chinh.

CHINH: I'm not a monster.

CHINH smacks the sand in MAI's face.

BẢO: Chinh. Stop misbehaving. You're the eldest son. Someday when I'm not here, who'll take care of your sister?

MAI: I can take care of myself, Ba.

BẢO: Family looks after each other. That is the Vietnamese way. We may not live in Việt Nam anymore, but we are still –

Pause.

Vietnamese.

MAI: (*in the present*) Vietnamese.

HÀ: (*also in the present*) Yes, the sand everywhere. The typhoon nearly blow us away. Two day later, police put us on bus for refugee camp. Life be better.

THE SEPARATION

The second Malaysian beach. BẢO and HÀ walk a plank to a boat. MALAYSIAN GUARD guides the refugees. HÀ slips on the wet plank.

BẢO: Em, take off your shoes, I'll carry them.

HÀ removes her sandals and passes them to BẢO. MALAYSIAN GUARD allows HÀ through, then holds his stick in front of BẢO.

BẢO: My family's on this boat.

MALAYSIAN GUARD shoves BẢO, pointing to another boat. HÀ watches as BẢO exits. The scene switches to the present.

HÀ: That the last time I see your father. (*pause*) They say, come here, you go on boat. Two hour to the camp. Then they separate us. You be together soon. The men they put on small boat and pull them out to sea. Then they say it our turn.

HÀ's boat is towed fast through a storm. As the boat bounces on the waves, the women and children scream, beg, chant, and bow in Buddhist prayer. MALAYSIAN GUARD points a gun in warning as they try to cut the rope. Finally, he changes his mind: he chops the rope and exits. Everyone exhales.

The scene switches to the present.

HÀ: After one day and one night they let us go. (*pause*) We drift for one week. Two hundred women and children. No husband. No engine. No food. No shoes.

MAI: They left us on the ocean to die?

HÀ: Yes.

MAI: Without our father. What did you tell us?

HÀ: Nothing.

MAI: Nothing?

HÀ: You never ask me anything.

MAI: We lost our father and you said nothing?

HÀ: You did not notice. In Việt Nam, your father always working. You not see him much.

MAI: Mom, this is why I have no memories of anything. I blocked it out 'cause I was obviously traumatized. You never thought to talk to us.

HÀ: Talk. What good that do?

MAI: That's the problem.

HÀ: Mai. I not smart like you. I look after you so we can survive. If you not ask, I not say. You hungry, only you ask for food.

A FRIEND

On the boat. KIM enters and offers HÀ a small bowl. Optional prologue: adding to the sound of ocean waves crashing and the image of a stark-white sand beach is an image of a patch of berries.

KIM: Chị.

HÀ: (*from the present*) There is young woman on our boat, very kind. She give us a little food: canned fish, rice. She use sea water to cook it.

KIM: It isn't much. Take it, chị. For your children.

HÀ returns to the past. She passes the bowl to each child. Young MAI starts to cry.

MAI: Má, I want more rice and fish.

HÀ: Mai, remember what it tastes like. Can you remember? What did it taste like?

MAI remembers as her present self, speaking her thoughts out loud to herself, as HÀ remains in the past, speaking to an unseen young MAI.

MAI: The rice was salty.

HÀ: Yes. And what else?

MAI: The fish was salty too.

HÀ: Yes. Is there anything else?

MAI: There was tomato sauce. Sweet tomato sauce.

HÀ: You're right. Can you remember what it tastes like together?

MAI: It was terrible.

HÀ: No. I think it tastes delicious. (*licking her finger*) Mmmmm.

MAI: (*in the past, licking her finger*) Mmmmm.

HÀ and KIM share a smile.

HÀ: Thank you. My name's Hà.

KIM: I'm Kim. (*indicating the children*) Are they all yours?

HÀ: Yes.

KIM: What are their names?

HÀ: Linh's the eldest, she's eight. Then Chinh, Huynh, Mai, Hạnh, and Nien.

KIM: Six children!

HÀ: Are you married?

KIM: Yes.

HÀ: You have children?

KIM: No.

HÀ: Oh. Well, that's good.

KIM: What do you mean?

HÀ: At least you're not a single mother.

KIM: My husband's alive. He's here.

HÀ: I thought men weren't allowed on this boat.

KIM: Danh's ... sick. He was wearing my shawl. I guess they didn't notice. What happened to your husband?

HÀ: Bảo was put on the other boat.

KIM: Oh. I'm sorry.

HÀ: He has my shoes.

HÀ points to her bare feet.

Where are you from?

KIM: Cần Thơ. And Sài Gòn.

HÀ: Cần Thơ! Bảo was born there. Not far from Sóc Trăng where I was born. We moved to Chợ Lớn when I was six. There's a good floating market in Cái Răng.

KIM: My mother sold durian there. We'd be on the river for hours. My brothers and I gobbled the extras when Ma wasn't looking. She pretended not to notice our durian breath.

HÀ: That would be hard to ignore. My children love durian.

KIM: They'd have loved my father's: "Tastiest in the Mekong."

HÀ: Your father's a farmer?

KIM: (*nodding*) Three generations. When we were moved to a hamlet,[20] he tried to go back to the farm. They thought he was Việt Cộng.

HÀ: I'm sorry.

---

20 The Strategic Hamlet Program, planned by the governments of South Vietnam and the United States, was a pacification program aimed to win the "hearts and minds" of the rural population. Rural peasants were resettled into protected hamlets to isolate them from the Việt Cộng.

KIM: It wouldn't have mattered. His trees were black, the fruit withered to nothing. Eighty years destroyed in two weeks. That's when we moved to Sài Gòn. Hồ Chí Minh City. You know that wasn't his real name?

HÀ: (*deflecting*) I don't know much about him.

KIM: Not many people do, except for the politics.

HÀ: I don't know much about politics either. All I know is during the war we were afraid of bombs. The draft. But now, everyone's afraid of each other.

KIM: Communism makes everything communal. It took away community.

HÀ: Being equal is supposed to be good.

KIM: Not if we're equally poor. We've never been equal. What is equality? Is it freedom? Liberation? Rights to hospitals and schools while they change our education? While they change our money till it's worthless?

HÀ: I don't know. I left school when I was ten to work in a factory. Sister Six was the first to go to college. She became a teacher.

KIM: (*placatingly*) I'm a teacher too.

HÀ: What do you teach?

KIM: Music. I've played the đàn tranh since I was five.

HÀ: How old are you?

KIM: Twenty-four.

HÀ: And no children ... your husband must want a son?

KIM: It wasn't the right time. Too much uncertainty – our jobs, Sài Gòn ... and now leaving. I don't mean ... You're brave. Have you thought about where you want to go?

HÀ: I don't know anywhere except Việt Nam.

KIM: Everyone tries for America. But we want Canada. If we're blessed with good luck.

The scene switches to the present.

HÀ: I not know what Canada is. I not believe in luck. Good or bad. But I not say anything.

MAI: I don't know why you never say anything.

HÀ: You Canadian. You different. In Việt Nam your grandma make all the rule. I learn not to say anything. Not even for my own son.

SCENE 9

CHINH

Sài Gòn, 1974, morning. HÀ and BẢO's home. Far-off sounds of war: bombs are heard sporadically, but ignored by characters in the scene. MÁ, BẢO's mother, is tasting a bowl of cháo (congee). HÀ enters.

MÁ: (*harshly*) Hà. This cháo is too thin. My son can't eat this.

HÀ: I'm sorry, Má. I'll make it again.

MÁ: No. I'll make it. Watch me. Learn.

HÀ: Yes, Má.

The scene switches to the present.

MAI: (*sarcastic*) Well there's a surprise.

HÀ: Vietnamese mother-in-law very picky. She not like how I cook, how I clean –

MAI: How you raise your children ...

HÀ: Yes, that too.

The scene switches to the past.

BẢO enters, kowtows to his mother, and sits down to eat.

MÁ: (*endearingly*) Con,[21] Hà made bad cháo. I'm making a new pot. It's not ready yet.

BẢO: The cháo can wait.

---

21 Son.

45

HÀ: What's wrong?

BẢO: They've drafted me.

HÀ: Again?

MÁ: It's the boy.

BẢO: Má. We've talked about this. Chinh's only two.

MÁ: And it's been two years of bad luck. Bảo's been drafted every few months since the boy was born. We can't keep borrowing to make it go away. We've consulted the ancestors. The boy must go.

HÀ: Where would he go?

MÁ: It doesn't matter where. Send him to the jungle. The longer he stays, the more bad luck he brings.

MÁ and BẢO exit.

The scene switches to the present.

MAI: That's why you sent Chinh away? Because Grandma blamed him for Dad being conscripted?

HÀ: It different then. Your grandma give away six of your father' brother and sister. She never see them again. She believe in sign –

MAI: Superstitious.

HÀ: (*pointedly*) ... and she very control. I have no choice.

MAI: She wanted you to send him to the jungle –

HÀ: I give him to Châu.

MAI: I would cut off my arm before giving Jadyn up.

HÀ: You not make that choice. I hope you never do.

WHALES

*The boat drifts. A Cham ritual dance, meditative in style,
is employed as a transition prior to the scene. HÀ and MAI are
both in the present; however, the action of the scene transports
them to the past: they remember it as if they are living it in real
time. As the memories become clearer, there is a sense of urgency
to their lines.*

HÀ: It night. We asleep. A bad storm come. Lightning. Thunder.
Everyone is scare. Think more pirate. The boat is –

MAI: Rocking. Side to side –

HÀ: It too dark. Then we see –

MAI: A group of whales

HÀ: Another refugee boat

MAI: Whales that came straight for us

HÀ: The people want to join our boat

MAI: A whale collided with our boat

HÀ: A man jump on our boat

MAI: Then another whale charged us

HÀ: He try to help pregnant wife come

MAI: We screamed

HÀ: Everyone cry no

MAI: It was too crowded

HÀ: Is too crowded

MAI: The boat would capsize

HÀ: Our boat could fall

MAI: Then everything went still

HÀ: Then their boat go away

MAI: The whales guided our boat

HÀ: That man guide our boat

MAI: Through the storm

HÀ: Through the storm

MAI: For two days.

HÀ: For two days.

MAI: They saved us.

HÀ: He save us.

The scene switches to the present.

MAI: Wait a minute. I remember the whales.

HÀ: No whale.

MAI: You were asleep.

HÀ: It another boat. Like us. Hit us. That man, he refugee. Not a whale!

MAI: It was another boat ... of refugees? Did we go back for them?

HÀ: They gone.

MAI: You said that man's pregnant wife was on the other boat. And he jumped on ours ...

HÀ: Many people on that boat.

MAI: We left them to die?!

HÀ: Nothing we could do. The man, he save us. He see oil tanker, put big water bottle on his arm, and swim. The tanker make a call to Singapore. Five minute later a big ship come.

MAI: (*laughing*) Five minutes? It must have taken longer than that.

HÀ: No, I remember. It very quick. Five minute.

Elizabeth Thai as Hà, Chris Lam in shadow, in *we the same.*

PHOTO: Emily Cooper

ACT 2

SCENE 1

SINGAPORE RESCUE

The refugee boat and a Singapore Navy ship are aligned in the water. The Navy ship has sent a bucket of cháo,[22] but a crowd of refugees block HÀ from access to it. KIM emerges with the bucket, then offers it to HÀ.

HÀ: Are we going to Singapore now?

KIM: They're not accepting refugees. They'll take us somewhere else. Have some cháo. Feed your children.

HÀ: No spoon?

KIM: It's cold. You can use your fingers.

HÀ cups some lumpy cháo from the bucket using her fingers, and offers it to NIEN. He hungrily licks her finger.

The scene switches to the present. HÀ catches MAI making an involuntary grimace at the cold cháo.

MAI: (*jokingly*) Cold and lumpy, mmmm.

HÀ: It taste very good when you starving.

The scene switches to the past.

HÀ: Have you brought some to Danh? It'll be good for him.

KIM: He won't eat.

HÀ: Still sick?

Beat.

---

22 Vietnamese rice porridge, similar to congee.

KIM: Chị, I need to tell you something. Danh is an opium addict.

HÀ: Opium? Here?

KIM: Not here. In Sài Gòn. We left so he could get away from it. So he could get better.

HÀ: How long has he been sick?

KIM: He was a musician for the cải lương opera. After he lost his job, he played at underground bars. Sài Gòn girls, with their motorbike-riding pimps outside. Anything you want to smoke.

HÀ: Opium.

KIM: He just wanted to play. One night, he didn't come home. He was missing for two days. I thought that was it, the Communists had taken him. My neighbour took me to the den. It was inside an old abandoned shop, looked like a dead end. But there was a small room, full of smoke. The smell was like ... rotting flowers. Men lying on bamboo beds, with long pipes by their sides. We found Danh in a corner curled up on a mat, with a smile on his face. His eyes barely open; he didn't recognize me. He didn't move. He'd sold his precious ghi ta for opium. My neighbour helped me pick him up and we got him home. I went back the next day with money for his ghi ta. He was lucky he didn't get caught.

Beat.

I should go. Bring him some cháo.

KIM lifts the bucket of cháo and exits. The scene switches to the present.

MAI: (*disgusted*) My god. How did he get on the boat.

HÀ: You no remember? He sick, wear shawl. But I think she sneak him on, like a woman. Kim very smart.

MAI: I meant an addict going through withdrawal shouldn't be on a boat! Around children –

HÀ: Mai. Many people on boat. Me, a single mother with six children. Kim, she a wife with opium-addict husband. Biên, she a prostitute. We the same now. Refugee.

We go in small boat to Singapore ship. We the last one. Few second later, big wave come. Sink old boat.

MAI: Almost too good to be true.

HÀ: True: old boat no good. New boat very good. There are six captain – two Indonesian, two Chinese, and two English. They cook three meal every day. We eat so much, they nearly run out of food. I bathe you with one bucket of water. Clean the sand, dirt, and lice. My leg is bad – you all pee on it because no place to pee. One captain bring me medicine ...

A visual memory: CAPTAIN enters with ointment and a thermos of chocolate milk. HÀ is unsure of how to use it; he gently rubs the ointment on her leg, keeping his hand still to calm the sting. The two share a brief moment, then HÀ looks away. CAPTAIN hands the thermos to HÀ and exits.

MAI: Chocolate milk ... it was the first time we tasted it. It was like candy. Sugary, milky, delicious.

HÀ: They use canned milk. Sweet, like in Việt Nam. The captain very kind. The other people are jealous ...

The scene switches to the past. BIÊN enters.

BIÊN: Hey. Washerwoman. I hear you get extra stuff from that English captain.

HÀ: No. Not really –

BIÊN: Ask him if he wants sex. With my Tiên. I'll give him a good rate.

HÀ: Biên. He's a captain. Captains are important men.

BIÊN: Those men especially want sex.

> *HÀ doesn't respond. BIÊN grabs the milk thermos from HÀ and sniffs it.*

BIÊN: He gave you this?

HÀ: It's milk. He gave it for my children.

> *BIÊN takes a big gulp of chocolate milk from the thermos, then spits it at HÀ's bare feet.*

BIÊN: This milk is no good. Make your children sick.

> *BIÊN tosses the container overboard and shoves HÀ, who lands on her butt. BIÊN exits.*

> *The scene switches to the present.*

HÀ: Oh. I have very much pain in my bum. Then I sit there. I have no one to tell I am hurt. I cry because I miss my husband.

> *MAI helps HÀ stand up.*

MAI: You never told me the story of how you met Dad.

SCENE 2

FIRST SIGHT

Exterior of a Sài Gòn textile factory, 1965. BẢO, seventeen, enters with a bicycle. HÀ, fifteen, is humming or singing – perhaps the ballad "Ngỡ đâu tình đã quên mình" (I thought love had forgotten me) by Lê Hựu Hà. She sees BẢO and stops singing, embarrassed.

BẢO: Hello.

HÀ: Hello.

They smile at one another, shyly.

BẢO: You sing well.

HÀ bows her head.

BẢO: My name is Bảo. Are you new?

HÀ: It's my first day.

BẢO: No! First day? You looked like an expert. Did you know how to make thread before?

HÀ: I've been working in factories since I was ten.

BẢO: What's your name?

HÀ: Hà.

BẢO: Hà. Can I take you home?

HÀ: I don't have a bicycle.

BẢO: You can sit here.

HÀ: What if we get thrown?

BẢO: Don't worry, I'll protect you. (*teasing*) We won't die *right* away.

HÀ mounts BẢO's bicycle and he guides them across the stage.

HÀ: (*from the present*) Your father take me home on his bicycle every day, for a few month. We do not speak. (*in the past*) Hi. Thank you.

BẢO: You're welcome.

HÀ: (*from the present*) I too shy. I not even look at him. Sometime I feel him stare at me when I working. I hide my face from him. Pretend I not see.

In the past, BẢO looks at HÀ and she turns away.

HÀ: (*from the present*) Minh, one of the younger girl, flirt with your father. She very beautiful. I not so beautiful.

MAI: Oh Mom, that's not true. You are beautiful.

HÀ: People say I have nice smile. But I not beautiful. I know Minh like Bảo, and I think he like her too. It make me sad to see him with her.

MAI: What changed?

HÀ: One day I eating my lunch. Your father on second floor, make big spool of thread. He tossing them down on the first floor. He see me and smile at me. I smile back ...

The scene switches to the past, inside the textile factory, 1965. MR. LONG, thirty-five, the factory owner, enters. BẢO is dipping spools of thread into dye. HÀ is eating hot soup.

MR. LONG: Bảo! Keep working!

BẢO quickly tosses a spool to the floor below, his eyes still on HÀ. The spool lands in HÀ's soup, spilling and burning her hand. HÀ shrieks.

MR. LONG: You idiot!

BẢO goes to HÀ.

BẢO: I'm sorry, Hà! Is your hand okay? Let me see.

HÀ holds her burned hand out to BẢO as he gently inspects it, without touching it. The scene switches to the present.

HÀ: (*from the present*) The boss, Mr. Long, get very angry with your father. Almost he fire him. When Bảo's brother find out, he give him beating. But Bảo not care. He only want to know if my hand okay. That why I love him.

BẢO exits.

HÀ: That why I miss him.

MAI: It must've been hard to lose him.

HÀ: I think of him but cannot touch him. It hard for other women too. But it harder for Kim who have husband there.

59

SCENE 3

DANH

Morning on the Singapore Navy ship. An owl hoots. KIM enters, panicked.

KIM: Is there a doctor here? I need a doctor!

HÀ: Kim, what's wrong?

KIM: Danh's not breathing. Chị: he's not breathing!

HÀ squats near DANH's unconscious body, feeling for his pulse.

KIM: (*frazzled*) He was vomiting all night – I fell asleep for a minute. When I woke it was quiet – I thought he's finally feeling better –

HÀ: (*flatly*) He has no pulse.

KIM: I know he has no pulse – Chị, he isn't breathing!

The scene switches to the present.

HÀ: Danh lie there. His shirt have blood and vomit. His body feel warm, his eyes open. But no breathing. One more owl hoot. One more dead body. One more time I throw someone on the sea.

The scene switches to the past.

KIM: Oh god oh god oh god.

The scene switches to the present.

HÀ: But God not there. We have no God.

Beat.

MAI: How do you ... How do you not have PTSD?

HÀ: What that? It not all sad.

SCENE 4

THE SHIP PARTY

Optional prologue: we hear ocean waves crash on a stark-white sand beach and see an image of Vietnamese children in rags. We shift to a ballroom scene on the Singapore Navy ship. Women dance with each other to an eclectic mix of 1970s pop music. HÀ, affected by the music, starts to feel it in her body.

HÀ: (*speaking from the present, but acting as in the past*) The last night, the captain make a goodbye party. Candle. Food. Music. Disco from England. Chinese and Indonesian pop.

MAI: That's quite a mix!

HÀ: For one night, we think we at a ball. We pretend we wear beautiful dress. Before war end, Vietnamese woman look very good. They wear miniskirt. Colourful áo dài.[23] Their hair like French and American movie star – long, short, curly, whatever.

HÀ stops abruptly, ending the movement in her body.

Then American leave and everything change. Việt Nam become colourless. Everyone the same. If you different, mean you have money. If you have money, mean you a criminal.

The scene switches to the past. KIM enters the party, carrying two glasses of wine and a ghi ta on her back. She offers one to HÀ, who accepts. The two women take sips of wine. KIM makes a face.

KIM: That's not rice wine.

HÀ: I never tasted it.

---

23 Vietnamese national garment, composed of a long, split silk tunic worn over silk trousers.

KIM: Danh called it "tears of the motherland." Liquid strength.

Beat.

KIM: Do you believe in soulmates?

HÀ: Soulmates?

KIM: Two souls meant to be together forever.

HÀ: I don't think about those things. We loved each other.

KIM: Did you ever tell him? Did you say, "I love you"?

HÀ: We don't need to say it.

KIM: Why not? Why don't we ever say it?

Beat.

KIM: I thought I could cheat Death this time.

HÀ: You can't blame yourself.

KIM: And Death? Is that God's making?

HÀ: Death is just a word that belongs in the past or the future.

KIM: My future died with Danh.

HÀ: You have family.

KIM: No.

Beat.

The Americans had their domino theory.[24] They didn't consider families. My father's death was the first domino. Then Brother Two

---

24 The domino theory in politics was that if one country fell to communism, the surrounding

was drafted. Brother Three joined the Việt Cộng for revenge. The shame of sons on both sides, choosing one for the altar, was too much for Má. At least she never saw the fall of Sài Gòn. (*bitterly*) I don't agree with you about Death. It's always present, lingering like a stray dog. It's our fate, as Vietnamese. The dominoes keep tumbling.

HÀ has an impulse to comfort her but isn't sure how.

HÀ: You haven't eaten. Let me get you something.

KIM shakes her head, then hears the music, perhaps the ballad "Trả lại em yêu" (Return, my love), composed by Phạm Duy and sung by Lệ Thu. Caught in a memory, KIM extends her hand to HÀ.

KIM: Dance with me?

HÀ, taken aback by KIM's sudden request, is uncomfortable.

HÀ: Now?

KIM: When we met you thought we'd both lost our husbands. Well now we have. I used to wonder why war widows danced together.

HÀ: (*sighing*) I can't. I don't know how.

KIM: I'll show you.

KIM leads HÀ in a waltz. It is poignant, as both women think of their losses. KIM exits. The scene switches to the present, as HÀ lets go of the dance.

MAI: (*incredulous*) I've never seen you dance before! I thought you didn't like it.

HÀ: No: I not good – too shy, too clumsy. Not until Canada, after you all gone, I learn to have fun, to laugh, to dance.

---

countries would fall, like dominoes. The United States used the now-disproven theory to justify its involvement in the Vietnam War.

MAI: We weren't allowed to go to school dances. Do you remember the time me, Linh, Huynh, and Chinh snuck out to a dance? You caught us coming in through the window. You were so mad. Me and Linh were grounded for a month.

HÀ: That keep you out of trouble.

MAI: But you never said a word to Chinh or Huynh.

HÀ: Boy different.

MAI: How? They got into more trouble than we ever did.

HÀ: That because I keep you safe. Girl need rules. Need to be protect. You and Jamie raise Jadyn different. She have everything, more than you had. You never need that.

MAI: I want Jadyn to have a childhood I never had.

HÀ: You not teach her to speak Vietnamese.

MAI: She doesn't need to speak Vietnamese. It's more important that she tells me about her day. That I know when she's happy, or sad.

HÀ: Why she be sad?

MAI: Mom. Kids get sad. We were lonely kids. Outcasts. Did you know we were bullied? Almost every day. I didn't have anyone to talk to.

HÀ: You have your brothers and sisters.

MAI: We didn't have friends. We didn't fit in. We didn't feel Canadian or Vietnamese. You never knew because you never asked how my day was. Not even once. You didn't even ask about my grades.

HÀ: I working at three job. I not have time to ask about your day. But I sign your report card.

MAI: You didn't even come to my high-school graduation! I looked for you. (*pause*) I would've liked to know more about Việt Nam –

HÀ: You never ask. I think you not like –

MAI: I was a child, Mom! –

HÀ: At least you not get hurt. I not like other mother.

MAI: Like who?

The scene switches to the past. BIÊN enters. She is drunk.

BIÊN: Hey. Washerwoman. You talk to your captain yet about Tiên?

HÀ: Biên. I decided not to.

BIÊN: That's because you fuck him, don't you? You think you fool everyone with your six children. I know a whore when I see one.

HÀ: The captain is a good man. Kind. I'm not ... like that.

BIÊN: Like what? Like me? Like Tiên? What's wrong with being a whore?

HÀ: I didn't say that.

BIÊN: You don't have to. I know you look down on me. You're the same as everyone else. Commies, Southerners: you're all afraid. Afraid to speak up. Afraid of breaking rules. Oh, I see *you* all right. But you, you only see part of *me*. We all come from somewhere. Even whores. I'm not a beggar. We left Việt Nam because I know how to survive.

HÀ: Tiên is sixteen.

BIÊN: Tiên's fate was fixed long ago. The pirate sealed it.

HÀ: You don't believe that. Don't you dream of a better future for Tiên?

BIÊN: I used to. Dreams aren't for people like us.

HÀ: You have a husband. Doesn't he care?

BIÊN: You're so naive. My "husband" is gay. You thought we married for love?

HÀ: Maybe not –

BIÊN: Let me tell you about love: I fell in love seventeen years ago. Broke my only rule: "No Americans." He left before I found out I was pregnant. Oh I had dreams. I registered as a mail-order bride, to go to America and find him. It didn't work.

HÀ: I'm sorry, Biên.

BIÊN: Don't you dare. I don't need your pity. Tiên fell in love with that guard on the beach. She needs to learn sex isn't love. Talk to your captain and I'll give you a cut.

HÀ: The captain won't pay for sex.

BIÊN: He's a man. Men have one thing on their mind. You know who has the real power? We do. We know how to show them what they want. We know how to take their power and make it ours. You know what, never mind. It's our last night.

HÀ: Where are we going?

BIÊN: Your captain didn't tell you? We're going to Malaysia tomorrow.

HÀ: Malaysia? Again?

BIÊN: Nowhere else to go.

HÀ: They'll let us stay?

BIÊN: Only if you're Muslim. They don't want any more "yellow people."

HÀ: (hopeful) So we're going to camp this time?

BIÊN: (scoffing) Even if we make it, people've been there for months. Maybe years. If you last that long. There's rats the size of cats. Four rats to every person. Contaminate the food and bite you at night.

Make you sick. You won't last a week. Don't worry. I'll take care of your daughters. Virgins bring in good money.

BIÊN stumbles off. HÀ speaks from the present.

HÀ: There no place for Biên or her husband in Việt Nam anymore, and they know it. But Biên a survivor. She do what it take to survive.

We hear BẢO's voice from the past:

BẢO: (*voiceover*) We won't die *right* away.

As HÀ speaks, we hear a cải lương song from the party played on ghi ta by KIM.

HÀ: I go to the kitchen and I take some thing: a thermos like the one Biên throw away. Fill with milk. The lid keep the rat out.

A visual memory: HÀ, carrying the stolen item, nearly runs into CAPTAIN. She is caught. He takes the items from her.

HÀ: The captain help me carry. Then he ask me to sing at the party.

HÀ sings "Ngỡ đâu tình đã quên mình." After a few bars, KIM accompanies HÀ on the ghi ta. They finish. KIM takes the ghi ta out to the deck and lets it go into the ocean.

KIM: Goodbye, Danh.

As CAPTAIN, the Singapore Navy ship, and KIM fade away, HÀ is left alone, still in the past.

HÀ: (*whispering*) Goodbye, Bảo.

SCENE 5

MERSING

A field enclosed with fences. HÀ and MAI, LINH, CHINH, HUYNH, HẠNH, and NIEN are crowded among refugees. There are three logs.

HÀ speaks from the present.

HÀ: They dump us in Mersing. Thousand people here. Kim, Biên go somewhere else. I on my own again. They give two noodle packet, fish. Log to cook but nothing to cut. No match.

MALAYSIAN GUARD enters, carrying a squash. He hands it to HÀ, then exits.

HÀ: One pumpkin.

REFUGEE MAN enters, takes a log, and exits.

HÀ: Before the war, people help each other. War change people. They take for themself. They push, they fight, they lie, they cheat. They not help, they not trust. Stuck in tug of war for thousand year. But Vietnamese know how to change which side they need, to get ahead.

The scene switches to the past. SMOKING MAN enters, smoking a cigarette and carrying an axe.

HÀ: (*to SMOKING MAN*) Where did you find the axe?

SMOKING MAN: You want me to cut the wood? We can help each other. If I cut this wood for you, you give me something.

Beat.

Cigarettes. You got cigarettes?

HÀ: I don't smoke.

SMOKING MAN: No cigarettes? Hmm. (*suggestively*) You have something you can trade?

HÀ: I don't have anything.

SMOKING MAN: You have noodles. Give me one packet.

HÀ: I used them already. You don't look Vietnamese.

SMOKING MAN: I'm H'Mông.

HÀ: You're mọi?[25]

    SMOKING MAN bristles at the derogatory term.

SMOKING MAN: H'Mông. You're Ba Tàu?[26] Chinese? Like my ancestors. Maybe I'm more Vietnamese than you.

HÀ: (*curtly*) I'm Saigonese. You're not from the South.

SMOKING MAN: I was born near Đà Lạt. But you're not interested in my heritage, are you? Go ahead. Ask me.

HÀ: Which side were you on?

SMOKING MAN: I fought for the South when I was fourteen. Diệm[27] put Catholics in the Highlands. Our Land. A father shouldn't play favourites.

    I believed the Americans, like you. But we were shadows in our own land, no different than with the French. One who drinks will drink again.

HÀ: You became a Communist.

---

25 Pronounced "moy," a derogatory term meaning "savage."

26 A derogatory term for ethnic Chinese living in Việt Nam. *Ba* means "three," and *tàu* means "ship." (An etymological hypothesis is offered here: Wiktionary, "Ba Tàu," en.wiktionary.org/wiki/Ba_Tàu#Etymology.)

27 Ngô Đình Diệm (1901–1963), South Vietnamese autocratic and Christian politician.

SMOKING MAN: A liberator.

HÀ: You fought with the Việt Cộng.

SMOKING MAN: I wrote poetry for our comrades. Collected body
parts of our brothers and sisters – a foot, a head. And yes. I fought.
I fought for the cause.

HÀ: What about the brothers and sisters you killed –

SMOKING MAN: We had to win or die –

HÀ: Innocent people –

SMOKING MAN: People aren't innocent. Not even your American
bandits and their puppet troops. But does anyone deserve war? You
know what I saw? Our countryside ravaged by napalm and Agent
Orange, words every peasant knows. I heard the soldiers' cries, as the
flesh was seared from their bones. And Mother Nature was the least
forgiving, with her tigers and snakes. I'd rather a quick bullet.

HÀ: Tigers kill when they're hungry. They're not savages, who don't
know how to stop.

SMOKING MAN: You think we're the savages? My village, my *home*,
was reduced to mass graves and ashes. Việt Cộng, Việt Minh, People's
Army, Army of the Republic – what does it matter. We all did it. War
made savages of us all.

HÀ: Communism took everything we had!

SMOKING MAN: Communism isn't the problem. When the tree is
fallen, everyone runs to it with their axe.

HÀ: You invaded the South!

SMOKING MAN: We rescued the South.

HÀ: Rescue? We didn't ask to be rescued! We were happy with
what we had!

SMOKING MAN: How could you be happy with divorced parents? A foreign stepfather with his broken promises? Did you ever think about what you were fighting *for*, rather than *against*?

HÀ: (*persistently*) What about your broken promises?! You promised to liberate us and treat us as brothers and sisters. Instead you jailed us, threw us in the jungle, took our homes and money!

SMOKING MAN: We weren't fighting for comfort. This was a moment born of a thousand years. It only took you twenty to forget, in your desire to be a fat American. Defending a country that wasn't really yours, that died in 1975.

HÀ: I'd rather be a fat American than a poor communist. But you got what you wanted. Why did you leave?

Beat.

SMOKING MAN: Every night I see them. Butterflies. I hear the ghosts, some buried alive, who won't let go. They no longer care about sides or morals or politics. But they won't stop screaming.

HÀ: (*to herself*) The baby haunts my dreams too. (*to him*) I threw a dead baby into the ocean.

SMOKING MAN: I just want a new life. Start over again.

HÀ: I want my old life back.

SMOKING MAN: (*sympathetically*) Are you alone? No husband? You and your children can stay with me. We'll help each other.

HÀ: We don't need your help.

SMOKING MAN smokes, thinks. Finally, he chops the logs. He uses his lighter to light a fire. HÀ slowly takes one packet of noodles from her pocket and offers it to him.

SMOKING MAN: Keep it.

He exits, carrying his axe. The scene switches to the present.

MAI: You had noodles.

HÀ: He Communist. Mọi. Some say they have tail. How he get out? Maybe spy. Smelly too. Everyone smelly. Sweat, waste, burning garbage and food. Hot and muggy. I a woman. Have my period and nothing for it. Many mosquito and fly. We get very itchy. There are fifteen hundred people here now. All night we lay like sardine next to each other.

The scene switches to the past. CHINH enters. MUSLIM WOMAN stands on the other side of the fence, tossing food over. She calls to CHINH, pointing to the food.

MUSLIM WOMAN: Dik![28] Hey boy!

CHINH bends to pick the food up.

HÀ: Chinh, don't touch that.

CHINH: She gave it to me.

CHINH points to MUSLIM WOMAN behind the fence.

MUSLIM WOMAN: It's food. Take it. I'm fasting for Ramadan.

HÀ: Put it back before the police see and beat you for it.

MUSLIM WOMAN exits.

CHINH: Má, she's my friend –

HÀ: We have no friends here.

MALAYSIAN GUARD enters, carrying a gun.

---

28 Boy! (in Bahasa Melayu, the Malay language).

MALAYSIAN GUARD: (*shouting names and butchering their pronunciations*) Ngô Trong Tri. Mách Vinh Toán. Chu Nguyên Đan ...

> *MALAYSIAN GUARD points the gun at HÀ. There is a feeling of dread. HÀ hugs her children tightly. They follow MALAYSIAN GUARD and, as instructed, board a refugee boat that is tied to a Malaysian police boat. MALAYSIAN GUARD exits. The scene switches to the present.*

HÀ: They separate the men again. Put us on boat. I nearly faint: they going to throw us away. This time we cut the rope. The Malaysians turn their boat around.

> *Beat. HÀ and her children are relieved as they watch the Malaysian police boat leave.*

HÀ: They go far away. Make more power. They come back. Fast.

> *The scene switches to the past. The Malaysian police boat turns around and charges the refugee boat.*

LINH: Má! They're gonna hit us!

HUYNH: It's not stopping!

> *The Malaysian police boat rams into the refugee boat. HÀ and MAI, LINH, CHINH, HUYNH, HẠNH, and NIEN stumble and fall. HÀ, carrying NIEN on her back, HẠNH in one arm, reaches for LINH as the children scream.*

HÀ: Linh! I've got you!

> *The Malaysian police boat turns away, then charges the refugee boat again. HÀ and the children scream.*

HÀ: Hold on to each other! Don't move!

> *HÀ holds on to LINH, HẠNH, and NIEN. MAI, CHINH, and HUYNH hold on to each other, crying, as the Malaysian boat*

charges a third time. HÀ speaks from the present in what follows, but the action remains in the past.

HÀ: I not scare anymore! If we die, we die together. I want to
die together!

> *The Malaysian boat finally exits. HÀ and MAI, LINH, CHINH, HUYNH, HẠNH, and NIEN slowly stand up and hug each other. The scene switches to the present.*

MAI: (*distraught*) They rammed us three times?! And the whole time
you held on to Linh!

HÀ: What?

MAI: You had Hạnh and Nien, and you picked Linh.

HÀ: She sliding away.

MAI: What about the rest of us?

HÀ: You there too. Sliding!

MAI: Mom. You always pick Linh first. You favour her.

HÀ: No, I not favour her.

MAI: Of course you do. All I ever wanted was you to love me as
much as Linh.

HÀ: Mai. I love all my children. Linh different: she the eldest. She
help me. But we all in danger still. Stuck on the sea again. This time
boat have hole.

SCENE 6

DRIFTING

The damaged refugee boat is drifting on the South China Sea.
The pace is languid, almost dreamlike, to reflect the hopelessness
of drifting on the ocean.

MAI: We drift

LINH: in a boat filled with holes

HUYNH: and water

CHINH: and people

MAI: refugees

LINH: on the water

HUYNH: in a boat

CHINH: drifting

MAI: without food

LINH: or water

HUYNH: or clothing

CHINH: or shelter

MAI: sinking

LINH: submerging

HUYNH: drowning

CHINH: disappearing

MAI: nobody hears

LINH: or sees

HUYNH: or knows

CHINH: or cares.

MAI: helpless

LINH: hopeless

CHINH: fatherless

HUYNH: Godless.

The scene switches to the present.

MAI: We were sinking. Linh was the one who suggested it ...

The scene switches to the past.

LINH: We have to be loud, or he won't hear us –

CHINH: How's that gonna work? –

LINH: He's supposed to help, when we call for him –

HUYNH: Is that it? Lạc Long! –

LINH: Not yet, Huynh. We have to do it together.

MAI: Should we close our eyes? –

CHINH: We won't see him. –

LINH: We'll call him three times. Ready?

MAI, LINH, CHINH, and HUYNH nod.

LINH: One, two, three.

MAI, LINH, CHINH, and HUYNH: (*screaming*) Lạc Long!

> *The call echoes twice.*

MAI: I don't see him –

CHINH: That's because Lạc Long isn't real.

HUYNH: Yeah. Like God –

LINH: Lạc Long is real! We just have to believe in him. Everyone close your eyes. Louder this time! One, two, three.

MAI, LINH, CHINH, and HUYNH: (*screaming*) Lạc Long!!

> *MAI, LINH, CHINH, and HUYNH look around, seeing nothing.*

HUYNH: Maybe he's dead.

CHINH: He can't be dead if he's not real –

LINH: He's real –

CHINH: Even if he's real, he's not coming. No one's coming for us.

> *SHADOWY WOMAN breaches the water not far from the boat. MAI, LINH, CHINH, and HUYNH do not notice. This should feel like a child's imaginary perception, involving the supernatural and blurring with HÀ's reality: the boat has reached shallow water, and the SHADOWY WOMAN tows it to an island.*

HUYNH: But we're his children –

CHINH: Not anymore –

MAI: Look!

MAI, LINH, CHINH, and HUYNH see SHADOWY WOMAN and believe it is Âu Cơ, the fairy. (Or is it one of the women from the boat, who gets out and helps tow it ashore? We are left to wonder.)

ALL: Âu Cơ ...!

MAI: She came!

HUYNH: She's beautiful ...

A rope materializes. The SHADOWY WOMAN seen by MAI, LINH, CHINH, and HUYNH points to it and disappears. Was she real? MAI, LINH, CHINH, and HUYNH work together to tie the rope to the boat and throw the free end overboard. It goes taut, as the boat starts to glide on the water.

The scene switches to the present.

MAI: Did you see the woman?

HÀ: What woman?

MAI: There was a woman in the water.

HÀ: Must be from the boat.

MAI: She disappeared.

HÀ: (*as if she didn't hear MAI's line*) Only women there. We pull the boat to Pulau Aur.

MAI: Where?

HÀ: It an island. Nobody live there.

MAI: You mean it was deserted?

SCENE 7

PULAU AUR

*On Pulau Aur, a small island off the coast of southern Malaysia.
Day one. The island appears to be deserted. NIEN is crying.
HÀ counts her children, holding NIEN in her arms.*

HÀ: Ssh, Nien, ssh. Linh. Watch your brothers and sisters. I'm going to
look for food.

LINH: Yes, Má.

CHINH: I want to stay with Má.

LINH: Chinh, I'm in charge.

> *MAI, LINH, CHINH, HUYNH, HẠNH, and NIEN exit amid
> CHINH's cries. The scene switches to the present.*

MAI: Linh was always looking after everyone. She used to feed us, give
us baths, brush our teeth.

HÀ: She good daughter.

> *MAI takes this in. The scene switches to the past. HÀ, carrying
> NIEN, walks to the edge of a forest. HÀ reaches to pluck some
> berries from a bush. A faint whistling sound. OLD MALAYSIAN
> MAN (an orang bunian, a supernatural being from Malaysian
> folklore) suddenly appears. He wears modern clothing – khaki
> shorts, a shirt.*

HÀ: Oh. Excuse me.

> *OLD MALAYSIAN MAN points to the berries and crosses his
> hands over his throat, indicating they are poisonous. He pulls a
> can of condensed milk from behind his back and hands it to HÀ.
> She looks at the can in her hand.*

HÀ: Thank ...

HÀ looks back at OLD MALAYSIAN MAN – he is gone, and whistling has ended. NIEN has stopped crying. HÀ looks at the can of milk, expecting it to be an illusion, but it exists.

HÀ: ... you.

HÀ walks back to her children. The scene switches to the present.

HÀ: I not know where he come from, or how he had milk. He gone before I can ask.

MAI: What did he look like?

HÀ: He look Malaysian. Beautiful face. Very old: he have long white beard. (*indicating her waist*) Down to here.

MAI: Maybe he was Indigenous?

HÀ: I never see him again.

MAI: Maybe he was a ghost!

HÀ: Not a ghost. An angel.

MAI: I thought you didn't believe in God?

HÀ: I don't.

MAI: The island wasn't deserted then.

HÀ: No. There are other men. From the mountain. Fifty men who come at night.

Night falls. The scene switches to the past. HÀ and MAI, LINH, CHINH, HUYNH, HẠNH, and NIEN are sleeping in a tent. From the mountain come shadows. Fifty men or so may be depicted through shadow play or through some other creative means.

Outside the tent, loud noises are heard: women scream as the men rape them and steal anything of value. HÀ gestures her children to keep quiet. MALAY MAN tries to enter their tent, trips on the empty condensed-milk can, and flees. The scene switches to the present.

HÀ: When morning come, they are gone.

MAI: Did they ...?

HÀ: They not bother us. They fall down outside our tent.

MAI gives a look of disbelief.

MAI: They fell?! (*mocking*) Were they old, too?

HÀ: Not all old people fall. They young.

MAI: And falling stopped them?

HÀ: He stop them. The milk can. Somehow they cannot get up.

MAI: It must've been an hallucination. A dream.

HÀ: No dream. It nightmare. Every night the same nightmare.
We protect by the milk can.

The scene switches to the past. CHINH and LINH enter. CHINH carries berries in his hand. HÀ grabs the berries and throws them down.

HÀ: Chinh! Don't touch the berries! They'll kill you!

CHINH: I'm hungry.

HÀ hands CHINH the empty can of condensed milk.

HÀ: Here, drink.

CHINH: We peed in that.

HÀ: Drink. It's the only thing we have.

The scene switches to the present.

MAI: It was urine?

HÀ: No water. Pee safe.

MAI: Urine, Mom. (*to herself*) We drank our own urine.

HÀ: Seven day go by. Then I see something on the sea.

The scene switches to the past. HÀ *removes her shirt, waves it, yelling for attention.*

MAI: What did you see? What was out there?

HÀ: Sailor. From Australia. He lost. Come to island by accident.

MAI: Thank god!

HÀ: He not understand us. He leave. Our only chance in seven day. And he leave.

HÀ struggles to continue: despair sets in.

HÀ: Ten day you cry from hunger. Then you stop. No pee left. You go …

MAI: We were …

HÀ: … quiet …

MAI: … dehydrated.

HÀ: … like that baby. Biên. Biên say I afraid of everything. She wrong. I no longer afraid to die. But she also right. I afraid of one thing.

MAI: What.

HÀ: I afraid to live.

HÀ slips into the past, crawling to the berry bush. MAI watches in horror as HÀ deliberately plucks seven berries.

MAI: (*from the present*) Mom?

HÀ cannot hear MAI. She is stuck in her memory: to feed her children one last time, and end the suffering. She picks up NIEN and calls LINH to her.

HÀ: Linh. Bring your brothers and sisters.

LINH, CHINH, and HUYNH enter, carrying HẠNH.

HÀ: Better we eat *right* away.

HÀ gets ready to give a berry to NIEN. In what follows, MAI continues from the present, while HÀ remains in the past.

MAI: What are you doing?! The berries – they're poisonous.

HÀ: Nien, be a good boy. Eat.

MAI: Mom! Don't give him that! You'll kill him! ... Oh God. You were trying to kill us!

HÀ pauses from giving NIEN the berry. HÀ cocks her head as if she hears something.

HÀ: Linh, where is Mai?

LINH shrugs her shoulders.

MAI: (*snapping her fingers*) Mom! I'm here! Wake up!

HÀ: We should be together ...

MAI: Wake up!

HÀ: ... for the end.

HÀ puts the berry in NIEN's mouth.

MAI: (*screaming*) No! Má!

HÀ is shocked back to the present as the adult MAI screams the line above. HÀ immediately plucks the berry from NIEN's mouth and throws it on the ground. We hear the faint sound of a speedboat.

HÀ: Mai? Where am I ...

MAI: Mom. You're here. You couldn't hear me.

HÀ: I not want to remember this. I sorry. I sorry. I make mistake. I not want to tell you because I no good –

MAI takes her mother in her arms.

MAI: It's okay, Má. You're all right. I've got you. I've got you.

HÀ buries her head into MAI's shoulder, as MAI soothes her. In what follows, HÀ and MAI's words blend with each other.

HÀ: I no good I no good I no good ...

MAI: Sshhh. You're good. You're good. You are so good.

HÀ pulls back from MAI. The sound of the speedboat gets louder.

HÀ: A boat come.

MAI: It's okay.

HÀ pushes through.

HÀ: From Malaysia.

MAI: You don't have to finish, Mom.

HÀ: (*firmly*) I want to finish.

MAI nods.

HÀ: Malaysia Red Crescent[29] save us. They good. Send navy boat to take us to Pulau Tengah. You want to hear about camp?

MAI nods.

---

29 The Malaysian Red Crescent Society, or Bulan Sabit Merah Malaysia, is the Malay chapter of the International Red Cross and Red Crescent Movement.

SCENE 8

PULAU TENGAH

*Pulau Tengah, an island west of Pulau Aur, closer to the
Malaysian east coast. It is a refugee camp, with primitive log
cabins, tents, and stalls. It is similar to the streets of Sài Gòn
we witnessed at the beginning of the play:"Little Sài Gòn"
in a refugee camp. Refugees engage in a crowded marketplace,
buying and selling. Rats run rampant. The air smells of cooked
food, sweat, and raw sewage. There is a monkey cage with
REFUGEE MAN inside.*

HÀ: (*speaking from the present*) Every day we wait. Life of a refugee.
We wait for food. We wait for interview. We wait to be accept. We wait
and wait and wait.

The scene switches to the past. MR. LONG enters.

MR. LONG: Hà? You worked for me, making thread.

HÀ: Mr. Long? Ông chủ,[30] I'm glad to see you! What happened?

MR. LONG: The government took the factory. We left six months ago.

HÀ: Even you.

MR. LONG: No matter what I gave up, I'll always be Chinese
bourgeoisie in their eyes.

HÀ: I'm surprised you remember me.

MR. LONG: You sang beautifully. And then there was the time Bảo
burned your hand.

MR. LONG laughs. HÀ looks down.

---

30 Boss.

MR. LONG: Hà?

HÀ: Bảo didn't make it.

MR. LONG: I'm sorry. You're lucky you survived.

HÀ: How are we lucky? Bảo's gone. Ten families in one cabin. Everyone
has diarrhea. Yesterday my son Chinh fell into a well. He's okay,
a neighbour saved him. But I wasn't there. I'd gone to get food. Two
hours, barefoot in the rain.

> *MR. LONG removes his shoes and puts them down in
> front of HÀ.*

MR. LONG: Take them.

HÀ: Ông chủ, I can't take your shoes.

> *MR. LONG insists and puts money into HÀ's hand.*

MR. LONG: Our connections outside Việt Nam send us money. Use it
to buy what you need: extra fruit, rice. Everything possible. They even
sell homes! Sài Gòn may have fallen, but we carry it (*pointing to his
heart*) here. You must have hope, Hà.

> *REFUGEE MAN in the monkey cage tries to get MR. LONG and
> HÀ's attention.*

HÀ: Why's he in a cage?

MR. LONG: They call it the monkey house. (*laughing*) They use it to
enforce the rules. He got drunk on homemade pineapple brew. It's
illegal, but they keep making it.

HÀ: You said they sell homes here?

MR. LONG: You can buy them with gold.

HÀ: Bảo had all the gold.

MR. LONG exits. VISA OFFICER enters, carrying blue index cards. A relieved REFUGEE MAN is accepted, then exits. HÀ takes their place.

VISA OFFICER: (*friendly*) How old are you?

HÀ: I'm thirty. I was twenty-nine when we left.

VISA OFFICER: When did you leave?

HÀ: We left in May.

VISA OFFICER: How many in your family?

HÀ: I have six children. We're on our own.

VISA OFFICER: Where is your husband?

HÀ: We got separated in Malaysia.

VISA OFFICER: (*concerned*) You don't know where he is?

HÀ: There was a storm. He's gone. I want to go to Canada. Where my friend Kim is going.

VISA OFFICER: (*sympathetically*) Sorry, you won't get to choose. There's one problem: we need proof of your husband's death before we can accept you.

HÀ moves downstage as VISA OFFICER interviews another REFUGEE WOMAN. HÀ speaks from the present as she repeats a mundane action, such as tying and untying MAI's hair in a ponytail, to symbolize the "Groundhog Day" feeling of life in the camps.

HÀ: Every day we wait. Life of a refugee. We wait for food. We wait for interview. We wait to be accept. We wait and wait and wait.

Every night I dream of the dead baby. She has Bảo's face.

REFUGEE WOMAN being interviewed by VISA OFFICER is not accepted. She bangs her head on the table three times before another refugee, acting as SECURITY, intervenes and leads her away. HÀ takes her place.

VISA OFFICER: Hà? You arrived nine months ago? We finally have proof of your husband.

HÀ: Where?

VISA OFFICER: Indonesia.

HÀ: Are you sure it's him?

VISA OFFICER: The records match. (*partly to themself*) The boat was severely damaged, in pieces. Must've been a horrific storm. (*to HÀ*) They took a photograph. We need you to confirm it's your husband, please.

HÀ shakes her head, holding back her tears.

HÀ: No. I can't.

VISA OFFICER: Hà? I meant we found him in a refugee camp.

HÀ: Refugee camp? That means he's –

VISA OFFICER: (*joyfully*) Alive! Yes! You'll be reunited with your husband in Canada! Your sponsor is a church. First, you go to Kuala Lumpur. Sister Monica runs our transit camp there. They'll do medical checks, make sure you don't have TB.

HÀ: Oh! Thank you! Thank you! A church. Do they know we're Buddhist? Do we have to become Christian?

VISA OFFICER: (*smiling*) Not at all.

VISA OFFICER exits.

HÀ: I cannot believe it. After one year! Bảo. Alive!

In the present, HÀ and MAI, both overcome with emotion,
embrace each other.

MAI: How did they find him? I mean, there was no Instagram,
  no Facebook.

HÀ: The officer make card. They find him! They match my card to his.

MAI: Incredible! All that time, he was in Indonesia?

HÀ: For one day and one night they tow us all closer to Singapore,
  so we can live. Your father's boat meet a fisherman; they help them go
  to Indonesia. Your father have all the money, all the food. He okay!
  He find a job at camp. Make noodle. Drink beer. He living the good
  life. While we starve to death.

  The song "Biển nhớ" (Sea of remembrance) by Trịnh
  Công Sơn plays.

CANADA

HÀ speaks from the present.

HÀ: Our first time on airplane. Full of Vietnamese fly to Canada. Canada, where Kim want to go. Did she make it? It very noisy, my ear hurt. How the plane stay in the air? I not look out the window. We hear it cold in Canada, we going to freeze to death. I wonder if Bảo freeze to death somewhere.

We get off the plane. Everyone sponsor come but us. All night we wait. Then they say: this Vancouver. We suppose to stay on the plane for Victoria! It sound the same. The next morning, we fly again. This time, I look out the window. And then I look down. I see tree. Mountain. And the sea. They going to drop us in the sea!

1980. HÀ and her children arrive in Victoria, BC. No one is there to meet them. Finally, BẢO enters, carrying HÀ's shoes. HÀ does not recognize him as he walks towards her.

BẢO: Hà!

HÀ does a double take.

HÀ: Bảo.

BẢO and HÀ share a long embrace. HÀ sees the shoes.

HÀ: My shoes. You kept them …

BẢO kneels, removes her sandals, and rubs her feet tenderly, in a symbolic gesture of washing the past away. He attempts to put HÀ's feet in her shoes.

HÀ: They don't fit.

HÀ has a sudden overwhelming urge to cry. BẢO comforts her.

BẢO: We'll find new shoes, em. We made it. Didn't I say we wouldn't die *right* away?

HÀ manages a tearful smile. MAI, LINH, CHINH, HUYNH, HẠNH, and NIEN, shy, stare at BẢO.

HÀ: Children, say hello to your father.

HÀ gently nudges LINH, who takes a step forward.

LINH: Ba? You look thin!

BẢO laughs.

BẢO: That's because rice is hard to find, Linh. Don't worry. When I find it, we'll buy so much, we'll never run out again. I promise.

MAI, LINH, HUYNH, HẠNH, and NIEN go to him, but not CHINH.

MAI: Chinh. It's Ba.

BẢO: This is your new home, Chinh. Canada. What do you think?

CHINH: I don't want another home, Má! Don't give me away again!

HÀ: Chinh. Your home is with us. Nobody is being sent away ever again.

HÀ gives BẢO a look that shows she's in control. BẢO opens his arms, hugging his family together.

FINALE

The present day. MAI returns to her recording from the beginning of the play, addressing the audience directly.

MAI: We made it to Canada on April 30, 1980, five years after the fall of Sài Gòn. Our church sponsor hired my dad as a janitor. Canada slowly became home. Mom took English classes at night. The first phrase she learned was –

HÀ: "A cup of tea."

MAI: Years later Linh met a boy from Edmonton. They didn't remember, but it turned out they'd been friends in camp. They fell in love and married. Chinh became a pastor at the church. To this day, Dad hoards rice; there's at least sixty bags in the garage.

    HÀ smiles.

HÀ: Your father keep his promise.

MAI: This is our boat people story.

    MAI turns to HÀ.

MAI: How did you do it? If I was in your shoes ...

HÀ: I not have shoe either. We not alone. We have help. Kim, the captain, Mr. Long. Even Biên.

MAI: And Linh.

HÀ: Yes, Linh.

MAI: (*slowly*) She was Jadyn's age. Jadyn wouldn't have the first clue.

HÀ: Jadyn know how to do thing herself.

MAI: She's only eight, Mom.

HÀ: You survive the sea when you four.

MAI: (*realizing*) I survived the sea when I was four ...

HÀ nods knowingly.

HÀ: She like you. Stubborn too.

MAI and HÀ laugh. A pause.

MAI: I wish I'd helped more. Asked about Việt Nam. Learned from you.

HÀ: What good it do? Cannot change past. I wish I help you when you little. Teach you to cook. Ask you, "How is your day?"

Beat.

MAI: How do you know, when to protect, when to let go? How much to sacrifice? How do I know if I'm a good mother?

HÀ: Mai. You are my daughter. If you not good, I not good. A mother know herself by her children: Jadyn very loving and kind.

Every day we make choice for our children. Now you decide. You tell Jadyn all?

MAI: Knowledge is power.

HÀ: It used to be. Power. Everyone want power. That what Biên talking about. The fight for power. But power not come from being smart. It come from gun. Smart people not want use the gun.

Beat.

MAI: You were smart – to give Chinh to Auntie Six. You knew Grandma would've sent him to the jungle. We'd have never seen him again. You protected him.

HÀ: He protect us. I never want leave Việt Nam. But I want Chinh back so much that I agree.

We hear the sound of bamboo sticks being shaken as HÀ slowly recounts the next memory.

HÀ: Before we leave, I go to temple. I want to know the future. The monk not want to read, say "no good." He say we go on long journey and your father will separate from us, and he die. But if we stay together, and our ancestor good, maybe he come back after one year. Without Chinh, we not all together. You understand?

MAI nods slowly.

HÀ: Have a plum. Vietnamese. I buy from Chinatown. You know your Chinese name mean "plum"?

MAI: Yes.

HÀ: You like? Not like Việt Nam. Good fruit there.

MAI: It's yummy.

As HÀ remembers Việt Nam, we hear the sounds of nature: the birds, the river.

HÀ: In Sóc Trăng, we pick fruit from tree. Until the sun set. Beautiful on the river. Your auntie uncle chase me with durian. Mangosteen –

MAI: Mangosteen ...

HÀ: Mangosteen your favourite. On good day we buy fresh from market. You remember? Sweet and sour – what you say, "joot-sy"? The joot slide down your chin.

MAI stops herself from correcting her mom. She laughs.

MAI: Sounds messy!

HÀ laughs with MAI.

HÀ: I try to clean but you say, "Má, I like it."

MAI: There is one recipe I can't google. Your phở. I'd like to teach Jadyn how to make it. Do you think you could ...

HÀ: I take you to Việt Nam.

HÀ makes a tender physical gesture towards MAI.

HÀ: We do it together.

In the background emerge photos of Vietnamese refugee families, along with songs like Lê Hựu Hà's "Ngỡ đâu tình đã quên mình" or Quỳnh Anh's "Hello Vietnam."

THE END

ACKNOWLEDGMENTS

I am indebted to Jean, May, and the Truong Family, my second family, whose story inspired the writing of this play. I'll forever cherish their friendship, unwavering support, and immeasurable consultation throughout the play's development and beyond.

Thank you to Kevin Williams, Catriona Strang, Charles Simard, Leslie Smith, Chloë Filson, and Talonbooks for choosing to publish this story, the astute edits, and for their incredible support of this first-time playwright.

To Deepa Mehta, you are an inspiration who I respect, love, and admire. Quite simply, you are my other mother: thank you for your support and belief in me, and for your insightful words on the play.

I gratefully acknowledge the following people for their contributions and support:

Andrew Wylie and the Wylies, O. Kashyap, Rita Malik, and Gautam Kapoor.

Dramaturgy: Rachel Ditor and Heidi Taylor.

Cultural consultants: Stella Nhung Davis, Nguyễn Minh Ngọc, and Tammy Lê-Son.

Script development and support: Donna Yamamoto (Vancouver Asian Canadian Theatre*), Heather Redfern (Vancouver East Cultural Centre*), Jaya Maruthan, Dato' Sayed Rahman, and Hj. Misnan (Malaysian Red Crescent Society), David Smukler, Michael Molloy, Donald Cameron, Trần Quốc Toản, Elizabeth Thai, Zakia Aris (United Nations High Commissioner for Refugees), Sister Agnes Ng (Infant Jesus Sisters Convent), Eddin Khoo, Chin San Sooi, Pearly Chua, Alvin Looi, Vivienne Oon, Tan Li Yang, Yiky Chew, Alex Ping, Hj. Badrol Hisham Zaki, Marion D'Cruz (Five Arts Centre), Wazir Jahan Karim, Charlie Wu, Margaret Tebutt, Nhi Do, Christopher Lam, Quynh Mi, Brandy Le, Khaira Ledeyo, Grace Le, Vi An Diep, Damon Bradly Jang, Agnes Tong, Melissa Oei, Lissa Neptuno, Connor Wylie, Manami Hara, Marion Landers, Mark Parlett, Louisa Phung, Johnson Phan, Jessica Fortner, Leanne Gillespie, Tom Woods, Lydia Lovison, Amélie Thuy Nguyễn, Nguyễn Hữu Đạt, Tami Do, Hamoudi Saleh Baratta (formerly known as Mohammed Alsaleh), Saleem Spindari, Stanley Chia, Rikki Bahar, Amy Ash, Devyani Saltzman, Rebecca Burton (Playwrights Guild of Canada), Playwrights Theatre Centre, Vancouver Fringe Festival, Canadian Play Thing, Terry Hunter and Savannah Walling (Heart of the City

Festival, Vancouver Moving Theatre*), Tari' 19 Festival (ASWARA University in Malaysia), National Asian Heritage Month Symposium '20 (Festival Accès Asie), and T-H Le; as well as the many people who contributed from Việt Nam, Malaysia, the Philippines, and Canada.

I initiated relationships with many community partners for the premiere production. In addition to those named above, I appreciated the support of: Anh and Chi restaurant, Immigrant Services Society of BC, MOSAIC (Multi-lingual Orientation Service Association for Immigrant Communities), Pacific Canadian Heritage Centre – Museum of Migration, Asian-Canadian Special Events Association/TaiwanFest, Vancouver Asian Heritage Month Society, and explorAsian Festival.

Big thank yous to: Dr. Benjamin Davis (Dean, Dalhousie Dentistry), Dr. Paul Witt, Dr. Terry Papneja, Dr. Elaine Lam, Dr. Dino Georgas, Dr. Ella Choi, Dr. Maneesh Bawa, Dr. Rajeev Sood, Dr. Joty Manocha, Dr. Nathalie Pauletto, Dr. Kim Mackenzie, Dr. Ron Melnyk, Dr. Crista Walker, Dr Nellie Trinh, Henry Truong, Mary Truong, Antonio Loy, Chris Lynn, Keilah Motola, Hira Ahuja, Shalini Kashyap, Mina Lauden, Harprit Ahluwalia, Sarah Dewan, Kusam Talwar, Frank Costanzo, Lynda Stokes, Trisha Takahashi, Elia Robles, Adrienne Fung, Craig Boyd, Denise Doyle, Jessica Morettie, Elizabeth Denham, and donors (too many to name) who contributed to the development of the script.

Finally, I gratefully acknowledge the support of the Canada Council for the Arts, Province of British Columbia and the BC Arts Council, the Wuchien Michael Than Foundation, and Scotiabank.

we the same was developed with funding assistance and support from Ruby Slippers Theatre.

Many thanks to David Edinger, Kailey Graham, and Madison Steenson for counsel and protection of intellectual property/copyright.

Thich Nhat Hanh, excerpt from "A Prayer for Land" from *Call Me By My True Names: The Collected Poems of Thich Nhat Hanh*. Copyright © 1977, 1999 by the Unified Buddhist Church. Reprinted with the permission of The Permissions Company, LLC on behalf of Parallax Press, Berkeley, California, www.parallax.org.

---

*   Including the creatives working within the organization who contributed to the play.

SANGEETA WYLIE is a Vancouver-based actor and writer with credits in film, television, and theatre. *we the same* premiered at Vancouver's The Cultch in 2021 and is her first full-length play. It received six Jessie Award nominations, winning two, and at the time of printing was on the curriculum at the University of Victoria's Department of Theatre. Wylie was shortlisted for the John Palmer Award (Playwrights Guild of Canada). A fully trained dentist as well as an artist, she has been a guest lecturer and clinical teacher at the University of British Columbia's Faculty of Dentistry, and she regularly volunteers with non-profit health-care organizations, in Việt Nam, and in northern British Columbia.
www.imdb.me/sangeetawylie